THE

MARBLE

AND THE

SCULPTOR

THE

MARBLE

AND THE

SCULPTOR

KEITH LEE

AUTHOR OF THE ACCLAIMED ASSOCIATE'S MIND BLOG

Cover design by Elmarie Jara.

Printed in the United States of America.

17 16 15 14 13 5 4 3 2 1

Library of Congress Cataloging-in-Publication Data

Lee, Keith Robert.
    The marble and the sculptor : from law school to law practice / by Keith Lee. — First edition.
        pages cm
    Includes bibliographical references and index.
    ISBN 978-1-61438-886-9 (print : alk. paper)
1. Law—Vocational guidance—United States. I. Title.
    KF297.L44 2013
    340.023'73—dc23
                                                                    2013036898

Discounts are available for books ordered in bulk. Special consideration is given to state bars, CLE programs, and other bar-related organizations. Inquire at Book Publishing, ABA Publishing, American Bar Association, 321 North Clark Street, Chicago, Illinois 60654-7598.

www.ShopABA.org

For Charlene, forever and always

CONTENTS

FOREWORD

by Scott H. Greenfield, author of the Simple Justice blog

I remember the first time I stopped by Associate's Mind, then just another law student blog to me. Law students. So little grasp and yet so much to say. My general take was that they would look back ten years from now and wince at their naïveté. But Keith Lee was different.

It wasn't that Keith knew more than the other law students. He was clearly bright, but so were most of them. What distinguished Keith, even then, was his focus on hard work, integrity, and perseverance. Where others whined, Keith worked. When others gave up, Keith worked harder.

As Keith describes in the pages that follow, these are tough times for young lawyers. Whether and how that will change in the future remains to be seen, but as long as law schools churn out more JD's than society can absorb, most laden with debt, limited skills, and an attitude problem, times will remain tough. If you expect things to be different, whether because you're special or because mommy said so, you're in for a rude awakening.

Many of the young lawyers who didn't have the opportunity to read a book like this before taking the blind leap into the abyss of the legal profession are bitter. They feel cheated. They feel abused. They feel that they were fed a pile of lies and left to choke on them. And indeed, there is damn good reason for them to feel this way. Unfortunately, it's too late for them to cry over their poor choice.

And that's where Keith excels. Wasting time, effort, and angst on blaming others for your misery gets you nowhere. Let's assume, arguendo, that you are spot on in blaming law schools, law profs, the ABA, your parents, all boomers known and unknown. Now what? Do you sit in the basement and curse them under your breath, or do you get off your butt and make the best of your own situation? The former may be easier and more fun, but the latter gives you at least the chance of success.

This book is about nuts and bolts, from the perspective of a relatively new lawyer who may be only a step or two ahead of you, but who has figured out that it's better to light a candle than curse the darkness. Keith gives you a match.

I suspect that his advice and experience, and even his language, will better suit your needs than that of a greybeard like me. Even if I said the exact same thing as Keith, it would come off like a lecture from your father or your boss. This is too important for you to ignore.

But make no mistake, Keith's perspective is neither one of a new lawyer nor old lawyer, but one of a lawyer who refuses to let himself be beaten down by a troubled profession and instead chooses to succeed. It can be done. You can do it. Don't worry about those other guys who can't be bothered reading this book and would rather complain about the misery of their lives.

By getting this book, you've already chosen to take the first step in seizing control of your professional life. When you're done with this book, you will realize that your success is up to you. While there is no guarantee anymore that becoming a lawyer will afford you even a moderately comfortable life, you can significantly improve your chances by doing the things that offer you the greatest opportunity for success.

Though Keith's advice is from a new lawyer, it's greybeard approved. You may not care now, but someday you will appreciate that a few of us old guys learned a little something along the way. And while I won't add to your misery by reminding you that the law is an honorable and learned profession, it wouldn't hurt to keep it in the back of your head as you move forward in your career. It's let me sleep soundly for more than thirty years.

INTRODUCTION

If you're a new lawyer in today's economy, you're probably asking your-self one of the following questions:

- **How do I transition from law school to law practice?**
- **How do I get a job?**
- **How can I find like-minded mentors and colleagues?**
- **How do I develop a book of business?**
- **How do I become a good lawyer?**

These questions are on the minds of almost every new lawyer, but especially now considering the state of the legal industry. These are the types of questions that weigh on you and keep you awake at night, along with thoughts like "Was going to law school really the right deci-sion?" or "Should I be doing something else with my life?" They are natural questions to ask. If you aren't asking yourself these questions—even if you have a job—you are ignoring the world to your detriment.

The entire legal industry is in a state of flux. Legal work is being automated, down-sized, and outsourced. The amount of work is shrinking as well. Clients have become more intelligent and scrutiniz-ing. Corporate work is being moved in-house. Contract attorneys are on the rise. People are turning to Internet services like LegalZoom or RocketLawyer instead of a local lawyer for "routine" work. Document review mills are bulging with new law school graduates who think they have no other options.

At the same time, law schools are flooding the legal job market with a glut of new lawyers, the majority of whom are unequipped, uninformed, and untrained to deal with the realities of the current legal environment. It's quite possible that you're one of them.

The problem is that law schools teach students how to think like lawyers, but not how to practice like lawyers. They have been miserable at properly preparing their graduates to function as useful attorneys after graduation. In the past, law firms and clients were the ones left footing the bill to train new lawyers—but no longer. Now law firms and clients expect new lawyers to be able to hit the ground running. Especially considering the oversupply of lawyers available, it is easier than ever for law firms to pick up experienced lawyers for low rates. As such, many new lawyers are left without guidance or direction.

I know this first-hand because I graduated from law school into this environment in 2010. Like so many others, I was dropped into practice when the legal industry was at the lowest hiring rate in decades. Although I was fortunate enough to get a job, I wasn't confident in my skills or ability to properly execute as a lawyer and effectively represent clients. This was a problem that didn't suddenly occur to me after graduation, but something I had been considering since my first year of law school.

So, during my final year of law school, I started a legal blog[1] titled Associate's Mind,[2] a play on words of a concept in Zen known as *shoshin*, or "beginner's mind." A "beginner's mind" refers to having an attitude of openness, eagerness, and lack of preconceptions when studying a subject, even when studying at an advanced level, just as a beginner in that subject would.

I wanted to adopt this mindset in my practice of law. The idea that an associate should be flexible and open to new ideas and processes, while being mindful of the guidance of those who have tread the road before them. So I decided to explore it in public at Associate's Mind, in hopes of building relationships and a community of other people who were dedicated to practicing law in the same way. While I had little in the way of expectations, Associate's Mind eventually grew into one of the most popular legal blogs in the country.

In the three years that I have been exploring what it means to find success as a new lawyer—what it take to become a good lawyer—it's become clear that the universal overriding trait among exceptional lawyers is a dedication to systematic, continuous improvement. The lawyers who are the best of the best are never satisfied with who or where they are. They contain an insatiable hunger for growth. It does

---

1. Or "blawg," of which I am not a fan.
2. www.associatesmind.com

not mean they are bombastic or unhappy with themselves, only that they contain a drive to better themselves every day.

Most people think they have it in themselves to succeed, to push themselves beyond their boundaries and shed their former selves and become something more than they once were. But they fail—again and again—dragged down by mediocrity and the mundane. Their failure is not drastic or sudden, but a subtle, grinding failure that chips away at them day by day. They do not have the fortitude or the will to push through adversity and boredom to fulfill their potential.

Yet there is another type of chipping away at oneself that is deliberate and meaningful. It is alluded to in the title of this book. Alexis Carrel, a Nobel-Prize winning surgeon and scientist, once commented:

"Man cannot remake himself without suffering, for he is both the marble and the sculptor."

This mindset is not easily adopted. It does not come naturally for many people. It requires discipline to dedicate oneself to systematic growth, abandoning things that might have once seemed important, and discarding patterns of behavior that may be entrenched. This is a significant transformation. One that many people do not successfully complete.

Your old habits, routines, and ruts; the same food, the same conversations, the same work; laziness, indifference, reluctance—are all aspects of your old self. The old you who adheres to the comfortable and familiar. Yet change involves effort, devotion and commitment. For someone who wishes to truly change themselves, they must embrace sacrifice. They must look at themselves and strip away parts of their old self.

Becoming a successful lawyer is possible for everyone. It is possible for you. You just have to want it badly enough. It has to become the overriding goal and purpose of your life. This will cause imbalance. It will interfere and intercede in parts of your life you once thought private. The separation between your personal life and your professional life will start to thin, to the point that it becomes illusory. And as any good lawyer will tell you—it is. Being a good lawyer is not a part-time job. It isn't something that you do in your spare time. It isn't something that you phone in or do when it is convenient. It isn't something that you fit in between checking Facebook and Twitter.

It's been said that, "An amateur practices something until he gets it right, a professional practices until he can't get it wrong." Becoming a successful lawyer, then, is a commitment to the transition from an amateur into professional—shedding what you once were and becoming more than you thought you could be.

Hopefully this book can help you on your way.

PART ONE
LAW SCHOOL

This book's primary focus is on the initial experience of lawyers as they leave school and enter the world of practice. But I wanted to offer a few thoughts on the trip through law school for those either considering law school or still in the thick of it. Even if you've passed the bar and are practicing, take the time to read through this section and compare it to your own experience. It should resonate as true.

If you have picked this book up in hopes to inform your decision on whether or not to go to law school, please pay very close attention to the next bit of advice. *Before you go to law school, go work in a law firm for six months.* There's no rush to go to law school; it will still be there when you're done. A shockingly large number of lawyers say something along these lines: "If I knew what being a lawyer was really like, I wouldn't have gone to law school."

Far too many people have no idea about what really goes on inside a law firm. All they have are idyllic, ill-conceived notions from John Grisham novels and too much *Law and Order*. The practice of law is a grind. It is hard. It is taxing. It can be lucrative, but achieving wealth through legal practice is becoming increasingly difficult. The prestige of being a lawyer is tenuous.

So, before you make the decision to go law school, read this book and see if it sounds like something you want to do for the next forty years of your life. If so, then go work in a law firm. Be a secretary, paralegal, runner, or file clerk—whatever you have to do to get a foot in the door. Then watch and learn. See what the lawyers (particularly the associates) do day in and day out. Decide if it's how you want to live your life. Only then will you be able to make an informed decision to attend law school or not.

DO NOT GO TO LAW SCHOOL

If you've picked this book up because you're giving some thought about going to law school, you need to be damn sure you want to go to law school. On that note, the first thing I am going to do is attempt to discourage anyone who is thinking about going to law school from doing so.

The practice of law is nothing like you have seen in the media. It is not glamorous. While there are thrilling moments and intellectual challenges, they are spaced between pushing paper and monotonous review of documents. It's a ten-hour day at your desk, with a brief fifteen minute lunch—that you eat at your desk.

"That's okay, I'll be making lots of money." Wrong. Take a moment and head over to your nearest web-capable device and Google this search query: "lawyer bimodal salary distribution." Take a good long look. More than likely you are not going to be making anywhere near that mythical six figures straight out of law school. You'll be lucky to land something in the $50,000–60,000 range—and you'll work your ass off for it. You might hit six figures some day, but it's unlikely that it's going to happen right out of law school.

At the same time, you'll also likely have something in the nature of $150,000 in non-dischargeable student loan debt hanging around your neck. But you're an outlier right? A bright shining star that will buck these trends and get that debt paid off not too long after you graduate. Consider this statement by Supreme Court Justice Clarence Thomas: "I wound up on the Court seventeen years after I graduated. And I made my final payment on my student loan my third term on the Court."[1] That's part of the price in becoming a lawyer.

---

1. Conor Friedersdorf, *Why Clarence Thomas Uses Simple Words in His Opinions*, THE ATLANTIC (Feb. 20, 2013, 10:12 A.M.), http://www.theatlantic.com/national/archive/2013/02/why-clarence-thomas-uses-simple-words-in-his-opinions/273326/.

If despite all that you are still interested in being a lawyer, I can also tell you that it is one of the most interesting jobs in the world. Solving complex problems and providing inventive solutions is immensely satisfying. And despite reports to the contrary, legal work is often very creative work. You will constantly be approaching situations in different ways, looking for ways to exploit or dismantle them. Also, if you are the type of person who thrives on competition, there is no better place in the working world to be than litigation.

You also need to be suited to the type of work a lawyer performs. Someone once said that being a lawyer is essentially doing homework for a living. To a large extent, this is a true statement. Being a lawyer involves lots of thinking, planning, reading, and writing. Time in court is diminishing. The vast majority of your time will be spent in your office, at your desk. But if you enjoy homework—planning, reading, writing—and can tolerate long term (eighteen to twenty-four month) projects, the practice of law could be for you. There is deep satisfaction to be had from seeing something taken to completion over the course of years. But there is more to it than even that. You need to be aware of the stress.

Of course, they never tell you about the stress. Professors and other students make a big noise about the stress to perform in law school. Get good grades. Make law review.

Just so we're absolutely clear: **The stress you face in law school is bullshit.**

It does not even begin to measure up to the enormous stress that comes with being a lawyer. The stress that comes from being a lawyer is from a different world. A lawyer is a collector of problems. A magnet that attracts only conflicts.

In law school you are only dealing with your own personal stress. Study for contracts. Moot court try-outs are next week. On-campus interviews begin in a month. How will I perform? What will my grades be? It's all about me, me, me.

You will still have "me" problems as a lawyer, but there is a shift in the questions: How will I pay my mortgage? Can I make my student loan payments? Where is the cheapest place I can get my suit tailored? Will I make my billable hours this month?

The difference is that you now have other people's problems layered on top of your own. Suddenly you're lying awake in bed at

3 a.m. thinking about strategies to defeat a 12(b)(6) motion. Or earlier in the day when you were going through 3,000+ pages of discovery response—are you really, positively certain that you found every bit of evidence that should not be produced? And not just problems from one other person. You will take on the problems of dozens of other people at once. Problems will pile up on your shoulders. And even when you're done with a matter, there sometimes will be a nagging doubt whether you handled the case correctly.

Yet if you can manage the stress, embrace the work, and be willing to put others ahead of yourself, you can find great success as a lawyer. If this sounds appealing, and you are prepared to devote yourself to a profession, then you should go to law school.

CHOOSE CLASSES THAT MATTER

Deciding which courses to take can be one of the more confusing things about law school. Certainly there are core classes that every school requires (Torts, Contracts), but a significant part of a student's schedule is left to them to determine. In reviewing the classes available to you as a student, here are some tips to consider:

Anything that starts with "The Law and. . ." can probably be ignored. "The Law and. . ." is code for the pet peeve project of whatever professor that is instructing it. It will likely have absolutely zero significance in the real world. If, by some stretch of the imagination, it does have applicability to the real world, it will be in an area of practice so narrow that only twenty-six lawyers in the entire country actually practice in it. And every single possible client that might need their services has them on retainer.

The broader the class, the more useful it is. Law school is designed to teach you to think in a particular fashion. Part of this process is learning about certain legal principles. Far better to learn about these principles in a broad, classical sense. Once grasped, it's easy to apply these concepts to multiple scenarios. So as opposed to taking "The Law and Water Boundaries," instead take a class on Equitable Relief. Once you learn how equity works in general, it's easy to apply it to water disputes or any other scenario.

Take a "Business of Law" or Legal Practice Management class. If your school offers one, take a class on the business side of a law practice. Learn about accounting, management, running an office, vendors, technology, marketing, etc. Even if you end up joining a firm and running the firm is (obviously) not your responsibility, such a class will give you insight on what it takes to actually keep the doors open.

Trial advocacy classes are a big plus. Any class that can actually get you in a courtroom scenario and thinking on your feet is a good thing. You need to get used to being pressured and performing in front of an audience, particularly an audience that is judging you. Judges will do it. Juries will do it. Clients will do it. Might as well get used to it as soon as possible.

Take every writing class you can. Then write more. High quality writing skills cannot be emphasized enough. Writing well is one of the most important skills a lawyer can possess. Writing is the basis of all advocacy and communication. Well before you enter a courtroom, deposition, or arbitration, you will have exchanged thousands and thousands of words with your client, opposing counsel, judge, etc. With a dwindling amount of cases going to trial and the rise of alternative dispute resolution, increasingly the only form of advocacy that is practiced *is* written advocacy. If you cannot write well, more than likely you will be a bad lawyer. (ProTip: You think you already write well. You probably don't.)

REPUTATIONS AND NETWORKING BEGIN IN LAW SCHOOL

Something that will likely be skimmed over on opening day is the importance of professional behavior, beginning now. Law school is not undergrad, despite the fact that a number of your classmates will continue to behave as though it is. Law school is a professional school, training students to become members of a profession with set ethical standards and rules. And you will be seeing your fellow students for a long time, because, more than likely, all of you will be limited to the geographic area around your school.

Law schools like to talk big about preparing their students for jobs anywhere in the country, but in practice this isn't true. Generally speaking, only graduates from the very top schools have that flexibility. Graduates in the top of their class from very good schools (but not the best schools) will likely have some of these opportunities as well. But in total, that probably amounts to 20 percent of graduates that law schools crank out every year. Which means that the large majority of new lawyers are being left to seek jobs near their law schools.

While you probably think "I'm different!"—you're probably not. You'll likely be getting a job, in state, near the law school you attend, along with the rest of your graduating class. This is why reputations developed in law school matter. Starting in law school, the very first day, you are developing your reputation as an attorney.

Whenever I mention that to law students, they usually get a puzzled look on their faces. Earth to space cadets: the other people in law school with you are all going to be lawyers too.

And guess what? Their perception of you in law school will carry into the real world. Party guy? Skip out on study groups? Late to class? Flake out on that committee you joined? The people you are with in school right now will share that with everyone else they come into contact with at their firms when your name comes up. "Yeah, I know Alicia! She did the longest keg stand on intramural day!"

The flip side is of course true. "I remember Laura. She was one of the most serious in our class. Always on time and prepared. Law review. A committed student."

The impressions you make on your fellow students are likely to last for years. And they will share those impressions with other lawyers in their firm when you are opposing counsel in a case, co-counsel on a case, up for a committee appointment, interviewing for a job, and every other situation imaginable. People talk, lawyers especially. It's in the job description. Therefore, it's imperative that your reputation among your fellow students is a good one. Beyond that, now is the time to form as many relationships as possible.

BUILD LASTING RELATIONSHIPS

While your primary focus in law school should be acquiring the skills to become a good lawyer, a secondary goal is to develop deep relationships—with students, professors, and alumni. While it might seem far away at the moment, at some point you will need clients. They do not magically fall out of the sky or show up on your doorstep just because you hung your shingle. Clients will not beat down your doors because you have lots of followers on Twitter.

Most clients, and usually the best ones, come from referrals and recommendations from friends, family, and previous clients. In particular, referrals from other practicing attorneys are likely going to be some of the best clients you ever have. Older, established attorneys already have referral networks in place. It's an uphill battle to get an established attorney to refer a case to someone straight out of law school. Instead, your most common source of referrals will be those you established relationships with in school.

To that end, while in law school: network, network, network. You should go to as many social events as you can muster. A big part of building relationships and networking is merely being present. By being a constant presence at social events, people will come to know who you are by default. And don't just go to the "fun" events either. Law School Ball or whatever other nonsense is nice, but really just an excuse to party. While you can attend these events, your focus should be on the more low key events. Especially if they involve alumni.

Meeting and networking with alumni is one of the largest open secrets among successful people. Alumni have strong affinity for their alma mater. When partners get into position where they can begin hiring their own associates, guess where the majority of them tend to hire from? Their alma mater. Also, if the hiring partners want to get the inside track on who are the best students/top performers, who do you think they speak to? Professors. Yes, professors do more than just make your life miserable.

A recommendation from a professor can make a big impact on a hiring lawyer. Beyond that, getting to know your professors will help you succeed on their exams. All professors maintain office hours. Oftentimes they will be in there twiddling their thumbs. Most professors are happy to speak with students, especially if you come seeking more than just an answer to a question.

While you should visit a professor during their office hours if you need help with the material, office hours are also a great time to get to know your professor. Ask them about their background, where they went to school, why they chose to become a scholar instead of a practitioner. Ask them about their research; everyone loves to go on about their own work. This will make a good impression on the professor, but it will also offer you insight as to how the professor's mind works— invaluable when it comes time for exams.

Focusing on establishing a reputation as a solid, dependable, ethical person while forming lasting relationships with students, professors, and alumni will place you ahead of the pack when you graduate from law school.

A TENUOUS BALANCE: FAMILY, FRIENDS, & LAW SCHOOL

Another topic that people don't seem to address often is the effect law school has on the people around you: your family and friends.

Your choice to go to law school will have repercussions on your existing activities and relationships. Going out, having fun, hobbies, and the like, which might have seemed like priorities before law school, are soon going to drop to the bottom of your to-do list once you've started school. You simply won't have the time for people that you had in the past. If you aren't careful, this can cause resentment and ill will.

Furthermore, law school will change who you are. That's the entire point. It's about training your mind to think about problems in a very peculiar fashion. Most people don't view the world the way lawyers do. And if it's true that we are the average of the five people we spend the most time with—and you are about to be spending lots of time with law students and law professors—you are about to undergo a radical change while in law school. It's important that you make sure that the people already in your life understand this. And it begins with managing expectations.

MANAGE EXPECTATIONS

Your own, your friend's, your significant other's. Law school is a major time commitment. Everyone around you needs to understand what that means.

Long hours of class and studying are going to become your top priority in life if you want to position yourself for success after law school. The competition in law school is fierce. While you might have been able to coast through college, you will not be able to do so in law school. Everyone in your class is likely to be a "Type A" person. And you are all competing for a shrinking pool of jobs.

If you want to be competitive in this environment, you are going to have to make sacrifices. This means going out less with your friends and more time spent in the library. And when you do go out, you should be going to networking events the law school or the local bar association is hosting. Your focus will not be having fun, but instead growing your network of contacts.

All of this adds up to the fact that much of the time you are going to be unavailable. The free time in your schedule is going to be sparse. As such, don't let the people in your life get the wrong idea about your time and be disappointed later down the road. Make sure they understand that you have made a choice in your life that is going to make strenuous demands on your time. Which leads to the next point.

COMMUNICATE

You absolutely have to have open and established channels of communication with those important in your life. I went to law school late (twenty-seven, ancient!) and was already married. I worked full time—forty to fifty hours a week and went to classes at night. After a year of law school, we had our first child. To say this was a strenuous situation is an understatement. If I had to pick a single word to describe it, I would choose miserable.

Not our son of course, who is wonderful, but my general state of being. The first six months after he was born is a complete haze. Work/school/study. Try to put baby to bed. Keep trying. Hour goes by. Baby asleep. Collapse in exhaustion. Two hours later, baby awake. Change diaper/feed/rock. Rinse/repeat at least two–three times a night.

I asked my wife, "If someone came up to you and told you that they had a spouse who was about to go to law school and they wanted some advice or idea of what to expect, what would you tell them?"

Wife: "It sucked."

But what made it tolerable were dedicated, open lines of communication. My wife and I made sure that we could be completely honest with each other. It strained our relationship—but also caused it to grow. We came out of the experience closer and stronger than we had ever been before. And it all came down to us making sure we could always communicate with each other on any topic. But guess what?

You will fail at this. Guaranteed. But that's okay. When it happens, take the time to sit down with your spouse/friends/family and genuinely communicate with them. Address any problems that have arisen and reset your relationship. Don't let things fester and go unaddressed.

KEEP YOUR COMMITMENTS

On that note, if you make a commitment to something at school, make sure you follow through. This ties into your reputation, but speaks to larger aspects of who you are. At a very basic level, people generally perceive a reliable person as a trustworthy person. Trustworthiness is the fundamental bedrock on which a lawyer functions. Without trust, lawyers are nothing.

Keeping your commitments is part of building that trust. This is not limited to law school either. It extends to your family and friends (who are also going to be your first sources of referral clients once you graduate law school). They need to be aware of your commitments and understand and respect them.

But it cuts both ways. If you say you are going to make the time to go to a family gathering on Saturday afternoon, do it. Don't cancel at the last minute to study Contracts.

SLEEP

Eight hours a night. Do it. It will improve every aspect of your life.

PLUG YOUR LEAKS

To borrow a phrase from James Altucher, plug all the leaks in your life. Like to go out drinking with friends? Surf the internet? Play video games? Keep up with breaking news? Anything that is distracting you from law school or spending time with your family is a leak that needs to be plugged. That's not to say that you shouldn't indulge when you have free time or keep up with hobbies or exercise, but the mundane things you do every day in your idle time are probably not worth it.

Those little time wasters that you use to fill up your day while you're bored will have to be cast aside. And in case you haven't figured it out at this point, here's a secret: boredom is a mask frustration wears. You aren't bored—you're frustrated. Frustrated that you don't have something meaningful to do with your time. Frustrated that you are refreshing Facebook for the tenth time this morning. Frustrated that your friends are doing something meaningful with their lives while you're stroking your iPhone.

Don't allow boredom to rule you. Take control of your life.

To put it bluntly, it's just not easy. Expect problems; expect breakdowns; expect disappointments. These things are going to happen. But you can either let them drag you down, or you can learn from them and use them as opportunities to grow. More than ever before in your life, this is a turning point.

You can either be a passive observer, letting the world direct the course of your life, or you can be a force of nature—imposing your will on the world around you and changing it to what you want to be.

Choose the latter.

THE FINAL PUSH

During your final year of law school, there will inevitably be an over-riding sense of malaise. Classes will be boring. Students and professors will get on your nerves. If you have to brief another case, you will want to throw the book out the window. All in all, you'll want to just push everything aside and coast out the rest of your time in law school.

Don't. Stay the course and finish strong. This will probably be the final year of academia for the rest of your life. Go out on a high note. If nothing else, it's good self-discipline in preparing for the Bar Exam.

Some students tend to think that, because they did well in law school, they will automatically do well on the Bar. Do not make this assumption. The Bar is a very unique test and likely very different from the exams you took in law school. Take the Bar very seriously. Over-compensate in your preparation.

Take a bar exam prep course—BarBri, PMBR, whatever. Devote two months to study and get ready for the Bar Exam. You only want to take it once. Don't leave anything to chance in your preparation. Get to the test site two days early so you have time to adjust and allow for last-minute disasters.

When I took the bar, I made it widely known that I was arriving two days early. Some people scoffed at the idea; others agreed with it. A fellow student, Ben, decided to arrive two days early as well. When he got to the hotel, he was placed in a smoking room—and he doesn't smoke. They couldn't change his room, as the hotel was booked. So he spent the night in a smoking room. Ben woke up the next day with a splitting headache and reeking of smoke. If he had to take the Bar that morning, he would have been miserable. Instead, he got his room fixed the next day and was able to have a good night's sleep before the bar exam.

That's a straightforward problem. The night before I took the bar, I stayed at a hotel one block from the test site. So it was full of law students. Guess who else was there? The Sons and Daughters of the

Confederacy Dress Ball. The lobby was full of people in period ante-bellum costume and uniform. It was beyond surreal. To say that it was uncomfortable for some of the students is an understatement.

With all that being said, I went out and threw back beers for a couple hours between the second and third days of the Bar. I passed easily. Your mileage may vary. But the reason I felt confident in doing so was that I had over-prepared for the Bar Exam. I didn't need to rush back to my hotel room to try and squeeze in more studying. Instead, I hung out with three other students I graduated with (all passed), drinking beer and reminiscing about law school.

After the Bar, be ready for a couple months of limbo. No matter how confident you feel (I felt pretty confident), there is always going to be a small doubting voice in the back of your head saying "Did I pass? Did I pass? Did I pass?" Just set it aside and focus on the day-to-day. Most people do pass the Bar.

If you fail, and have to take it again, it will probably seem like a huge deal. But in reality, once you are a year or two into practice, it will be gone from your mind. No lawyer cares that it took someone a couple tries to pass the Bar. I know a number of successful lawyers who did not pass the Bar on their first time. It has not hampered their career in the slightest. Clients never ask how many times it took you to pass the bar. It's not a factor in their retaining you as a lawyer.

Another thing that seems like a really big deal, but won't matter at all in five years, is where you went to law school. Law students have an overwhelming concern regarding the ranking and prestige of their law schools. To be fair, the ranking of your law school does have a large impact on your first job. Maybe your second. And it does matter if you want to practice in Big Law. But outside of Big Law and your first job, no other lawyer cares where you went to law school. No client cares where you went to law school. All they care about is: Are you a good lawyer. Can you handle their problems? Can you do it efficiently and effectively? Are you someone in whom they can place their trust?

If you're brimming with confidence in your answers in response to the above questions, it's likely that you're suffering from the Dunning-Kruger effect.[1] The Dunning–Kruger effect is a cognitive bias in which unskilled individuals suffer from illusory superiority, mistakenly rating

---

1. I was going to say you're a fool, but I'm trying to ease you into this.

their ability much higher than average. This bias is attributed to a metacognitive inability of the unskilled to recognize their mistakes.[2] Meaning that, because you don't know what you don't know, you feel confident in your abilities.

The reality is that, when you pass the Bar, you are once again on the bottom rung of the ladder. When you were a 3L in law school, you were at the peak of your educational development. Grade school, college, law school. You were a master student, excelling in navigating the educational world. But now you are entering the real world and you are a beginner again. A novice, a rookie, entering an entirely new field. Not just the practice of law, but of life. The support scaffolding of school is stripped away. It is now sink or swim on your own merits.

This time is difficult for everyone. If you have not prepared yourself accordingly, do not have family or friends upon whom you can rely, it is going to be an especially hard transition. But everyone goes through it. Every lawyer, every person you meet, was once as young, naive, and ignorant[3] as you are. It is now *your personal responsibility*— no one else's—to mature and develop into a competent lawyer who is fit to be trustworthy of a client's problems.

---

2. Errol Morris, *The Anosognosic's Dilemma: Something's Wrong but You'll Never Know What It Is (Part 1)*, N.Y. Times, (June 20, 2010, 9:00 P.M.), http://opinionator.blogs.nytimes.com/2010/06/20/the-anosognosics-dilemma-1/.

3. Yes, you are ignorant. No? Go read that bit about the Dunning-Kruger effect again.

PART TWO

FUNDAMENTAL SKILLS

There are simply some things at which a lawyer must excel. If these skills are not developed to a sufficient level of competency, a lawyer is likely to be a failure. Some of the skills discussed will seem elementary, and you might feel as though you do not need to spend time refining such skills. But to become truly proficient in any activity—law, swimming, computer programming—one must master the fundamentals. Elaborate structures cannot be built on ill-conceived foundations; they need firm ground and solid footing.

A new lawyer needs a complex and in-depth understanding of the rudimentary building blocks of the profession before they can begin to add-on more advanced skills. And these basic, fundamental skills will require constant refining. They are not something one addresses at the beginning of their career and never attends to again. Just as you will evolve in your understanding of law as you mature and develop, so will these skills. Some things that might have once been difficult will become easy. Other things that seemed simple to you when you were new to law may become more complex. It will be up to you to reflect on your development of these skills and dedicate yourself to improving them as you see fit.

ON THE IMPORTANCE OF STEALING

If you're fresh from law school, you might still recall Black's definition of stealing:

> This term is commonly used in indictments for larceny, ("take, steal, and carry away,") and denotes the commission of theft. But, in popular usage, "stealing" seems to be a wider term than "larceny," inasmuch as it may include the unlawful appropriation of things which are not technically the subject of larceny, e. ft., immovables.[1]

This is a fairly straightforward legal definition, but doesn't quite get to the heart of what it means to steal. The Oxford English Dictionary defines stealing as:

> [To] take (another person's property) without permission or legal right and without intending to return it.

This definition is an accurate description of what it means to steal something from another person. And I want to encourage you to do it. This might sound odd; it did to me when I was introduced to the concept by one of my mentors.[2] But stealing is an essential skill for you to develop.

Not in the context of actually committing larceny, but within the framework of learning and growth. When you are at court and have the opportunity to watch an excellent trial lawyer perform, you

---

1. BLACK'S LAW DICTIONARY 2nd ed. (St. Paul, Minn.: West Publishing, 1910)
2. Kevin Blok, *Kyoshi*. More on him later.

should steal. When you are at a topical, useful continuing legal education class (CLE) that covers fundamental areas of your practice, you should steal. When you read a book, treatise, or article that addresses ways to improve your practice, you should steal. When you encounter something that you know to be useful, that you know can better you, you need to take it away. While it might be a skill or idea or pattern that originated from someone or something else, if it will be useful to you—if it will help you grow—steal it.

Take these things, and never intend to return them. Make them part of who you are. Use them; adopt them; adapt them. Be greedy. Look for better ways to run a practice, write a brief, draft a contract, counsel clients, negotiate a contract, or take a deposition.

There is an old saying—"Don't solve problems, copy success." While this is not going to be possible for you as a lawyer—it is your job to solve problems—you are going to be able to look at other lawyers, CLEs, books, anything really, and steal their patterns of success. Because they are not going to give them to you. They are not going to force feed you improvement or development that can make you a better lawyer. No one is going to hold your hand and walk you through it. You have to steal it. You must have the active mindset of going out and taking the skills and practices that you want from someone or something else.

For some of you, this might make you feel guilty—that you can't take someone else's ideas, or that you know how to do things already and don't need to steal from others. If you feel the former, you need to abandon that feeling as soon as possible. If you think the latter, then you need to empty your cup and make yourself ready to learn. Better to do so voluntarily than learn lessons the hard way.

Regardless, **if you are reading this book, I freely give you permission to steal from it.**[3] Not all of it may be for you. But something, somewhere in this book, will resonate. You will know it to be true for yourself or your practice. When you encounter it, don't just nod your head knowingly. Steal the knowledge; steal the idea; steal the concept. Make it your own.

---

3. Attention literal-reading lawyers: Don't be cute; you know what I mean. This is not a grant of permission making the intellectual property of this book copyright free. All rights are retained by the ABA and myself.

WRITING WELL

One of the most important skills a lawyer needs to possess, if not *the* most important skill, is the ability to write well. Writing is simply the act of putting your thoughts on paper or a screen, meaning that writing is actually just thinking. If you are not actively writing on a regular basis, it is likely you are not thinking on a regular basis either. Oh, you might *think* you are thinking, but what you are actually doing is following patterns: routine and ritualized prescribed behaviors that you have built up in your brain over time because you are lazy. That is not a slight or criticism on you, but rather a statement of biological fact.

The human body is regulated by the parasympathetic and sympathetic nervous systems. The parasympathetic nervous system is responsible for regular body functions when you're at rest. Breathing, pumping blood, and digesting food are all unconscious tasks that are controlled by the parasympathetic nervous system. It does this to put our bodies into an energy conservation mode, sort of like when your computer monitor goes to sleep after there has been no activity for ten minutes. Thousands of years of biological development have made our bodies crave conservation of energy. Our bodies want to be efficient. To lighten the load on themselves.

The same is true for your thoughts. You go to the grocery store and buy the same things. You go down the same aisles and follow the same patterns. Milk, bread, eggs. You go to the checkout and engage in the typical, meaningless routine:

Cashier: "Hi. How are you doing?"

You: "Fine. How are you doing?"

Cashier: "Fine."

You sail through dozens of such patterns of behavior everyday, your brain on cruise control. Not actually being present and thinking through what is happening, but falling back on pattern recognition. This is not thinking.

Thinking is analytical. Thinking is creative. It is processing information and doing something new with it. Thinking is at the heart of what it means to be a lawyer. As such, you need to make a commitment to think as much as you can possibly handle, and then push yourself to think even more. While you might say to yourself that you will think while you're in the car (you're distracted) or laying in bed at night (you're tired), the best way to force yourself to think is to write.

Writing will cause you to organize your thoughts, encouraging examination and reasoning. It will hone your capability for analysis and synthesis. It will discipline your ability to process information and produce original thought. A dedication to writing well is simply a dedication to thinking well. This is of the utmost importance to lawyers because the primary form of communication you are going to undertake as a lawyer is writing. You will write to your clients, opposing counsel, judges, arbitrators, committees, and businesses. You will write letters, emails,[1] briefs, contracts, and wills. Writing will become a fundamental part of your day.

And while the best way to become good at something is to simply do it—you must resist slipping into routine and pattern recognition while writing. You need to be mindful as you write and not be satisfied with "fine." You need to take the time to learn about the craft of writing. Read books on writing. Take CLEs on writing. Go out of your way to read good writing. Not just good legal writing, but good writing in general. Read deep novels, periodicals like *The Economist*, and long form writing curation websites like *The Browser*.[2]

Expose yourself to good writing, learn about writing as a craft,[3] and dedicate yourself to improving it on a regular basis.

---

1. So many emails. Thousands and thousands of emails.

2. www.thebrowser.com

3. Suggestions on books and websites on developing writing skills can be found in the Resources section in the back of this book.

EVERY WORD MATTERS

Consider the following:

(1) Sally hates Mary.
    a. How likely is this because Sally is the kind of person who hates people?
    b. How likely is this because Mary is the kind of person whom people hate?

Sally hates Mary doesn't obviously supply the relevant information, but . . . numerous studies have found that people nonetheless rate (a) as more likely than (b). In contrast, people find *Sally frightens* Mary more indicative of Sally than of Mary (the equivalent of rating (b) higher than (a)). Sentences like Sally likes Mary are called "object-biased," and sentences like Sally frightens Mary are called "subject-biased." There are many sentences of both types.

Now consider:

(2) Sally hates Mary because she . . .
(3) Sally frightens Mary because she . . .

Most people think that "she" refers to Mary in (2) but Sally in (3). This is a bias—not absolute—but it is robust and easy to replicate. Again, there are many verbs which are "object-biased" like hates and many which are "subject-biased" like frightens. Just as in the causal attribution effect above, this pronoun effect seems to be a systematic effect of (at least) the verb used.[1]

---

1. *Findings: The Causality Implicit in Language*, GAMES WITH WORDS (Oct. 6, 2010) http://gameswithwords.fieldofscience.com/2010/10/findings-causality-implicit-in -language.html (based on research from Roger Brown & Deborah Fish, *The Psychological Causality Implicit in Language*, 14 COGNITION 237 (1983)).

If all of the above is a bit too technical for you, here's the distilled version:

Every word matters.

Even the small innocuous words that you might take for granted will deliver subtlety and nuance to the reader, whether you consciously intended them to or not. People have wildly differing viewpoints in regards to how they perceive words, systems, the world. You can't assume that people are going to read things with your perspective. People bring all sorts of baggage with them.

Weigh your words carefully and be cognizant of the way your audience will receive them. What might seem clear to you is often obfuscated or misconstrued by someone else who brings with them a different perceptual position. Slight alterations in phrasing and terminology can produce different interpretations by the reader. A single word can make the difference.

If you think that single words and simple phrases cannot carry complex and deep meaning, consider an example from a master, Ernest Hemingway:

"For sale: baby shoes, never worn."

Could you say as much in six words?

TWO WRITING TIPS FOR THE LITIGATORS (BUT APPLICABLE FOR EVERYONE)

AVOID HYPERBOLE

There is nothing worse than reading a brief that is filled to the brim with over-the-top exposition and exploitive narrative detail. It does not bolster your argument—it dampens your argument.

By forcing a reader to navigate sentimental adjectives and impassioned turns of phrase, you are removing the focus of the brief from your argument to your prose. While such a tactic might hold some weight when making an oral argument before a jury, it instead comes across as amateurish and impertinent when delivered in a written brief to a court.

That's not to say that you should avoid writing boldly or with zeal, but rather that any creativity in your writing should be expressed by means of carefully constructing and crafting your arguments—funneling the reader to a compelling conclusion.

More steak, less sizzle.

BE TEMPERATE

But what happens when opposing counsel resorts to hyperbole and bombastic prose in their brief?

Be temperate. Do not lash out at opposing counsel in your own brief. Do not waste words pointing out opposing counsel's flair for the dramatic or see it as a challenge that you must meet with flowery prose of your own. This is a fool's errand.

Opposing counsel has resorted to such language and imagery because they have no other recourse. If the facts were on their side, they would be clearly stated. If case law was on their side, it would be cited. They have neither. Hyperbole is bait, nothing more than an attempt to muddy the waters and draw you into an emotional argument. Do not be ensnared.

Instead, use opposing counsel's hyperbole as a foil in which to bring the focus back to your own tangible factual and legal issues. Address the overwrought language, acknowledge that it exists—but then move beyond it. When a judge looks at the two briefs side-by-side, it should be clear which is the professional and substantive one.

INSIDE BASEBALL AND GEORGE ORWELL'S SIX RULES FOR CLEAR WRITING

"Inside baseball" refers to using jargon, specialized knowledge, acronyms, or other such things when speaking and writing that will only be recognizable or understandable by a select group. Using shorthand is a shortcut to efficient communication among friends, colleagues, or other "insiders." But at the same time, "inside baseball" language is off-putting to people who are not part of the select group. It makes them feel like outsiders or perhaps embarrassed that they don't understand the language.

Could this be any truer of a group of people than lawyers? Lawyers are practically defined by the use of obtuse language. Dead languages, obscure references, and arcane phrasings are part and parcel of a lawyer's trade to most lay people. Yet, lawyers very often need to express complex ideas and concepts in motions, briefs, letters, etc. And often times the best way to communicate legal concepts is through the use of "inside baseball" language. Given the correct audience (other lawyers/judges) using a phrase such as *res judicata* is likely the best way to communicate a complex concept quickly and clearly because the writer and the audience are members of the same in-group.

Addressing such language to a client unfamiliar with the law only makes the lawyer seem intimidating or unfriendly. Instead of fostering communication with your client, it's actually obfuscating the matter. You need to know when to use "inside baseball" language and when not to. You need to really know your audience. Some people might like loose, casual language (clients), other might favor stilted legal prose (old school judges). It's your responsibility to know when to use which type of language.

Even when legalese might be necessary, you still need to use language effectively to communicate your ideas to your specific audience with your goal (education, persuasion, etc.) in mind. You don't need to use overwrought language; you need to use precise language. Your point needs to be presented naturally, your meaning clear. A good guideline for composing clear language was put forth by George Orwell, the noted British novelist, in his 1946 essay, *Politics and the English Language*:

1. Never use a metaphor, simile or other figure of speech which you are not used to seeing in print.
2. Never use a long word where a short one will do.
3. If it is possible to cut a word out, always cut it out.
4. Never use the passive where you can use the active.
5. Never use a foreign phrase, a scientific word or a jargon word if you can think of an everyday English equivalent.
6. Break any of these rules sooner than say anything barbarous.

If these rules were good enough for Orwell, they're likely good enough for us as well.

CHURCHILL'S FIVE ELEMENTS OF PERSUASIVE SPEAKING

Perhaps the next most fundamental skill a lawyer can possess besides writing well is speaking well. While writing will likely constitute the bulk of your work product, you will also spend much of your time speaking to others. You will speak with clients, judges, and other lawyers. Just as with writing, you need to be able to speak in a way that effectively communicates what you are trying to say. While much of the time when speaking you will be merely conveying information, the role of a lawyer is often to persuade.

Whether arguing before a court, negotiating a contract, or appealing to a zoning board, persuasive speaking is often why clients retain lawyers. Lawyers have to be able to speak in a way that brings others into their line of thought or their understanding of an issue. This is a subtle, nuanced process. A lawyer can't just hammer on a point and say "this is the way I want it be." While "because I said so," is enough to make a toddler follow directions, using the same method with a judge is unlikely to provide fruitful results for your client (and, depending on the judge, may find you in contempt of court).

For guidance on effective persuasive speaking, far better to look at one of the greatest orators of the 20th century, Sir Winston Leonard Spencer-Churchill. Churchill, famed British Prime Minister during World War II, was not only a noted statesman, but also a gifted student of oration and history. Churchill wrote numerous pieces on history, the English language, and how to develop the skills necessary to develop a mastery of rhetoric. So gifted was Churchill that he was awarded the Nobel Prize for Literature in 1953 "for his mastery of historical and biographical description as well as for brilliant oratory in defending exalted human values."

Churchill was a lifelong student of rhetoric and the art of public speaking. He was so talented that phrases and imagery that he used last to this day. Churchill's speech "The Sinews of Peace," in which he invokes the imagery of "an Iron Curtain" to describe the descent of Communism, which was dividing Europe in the aftermath of World War II, is perhaps the most notable example of his mastery of rhetoric and effective communication.

But in 1897, long before Churchill was Prime Minister, before politics and war, Churchill wrote out what he believed were the five principle elements of effective persuasive speaking in an unpublished essay, "The Scaffolding of Rhetoric." Churchill pulled these elements from a study ranging from classical Greek works to Shakespeare and Lincoln (who was himself a masterful student of rhetoric). These elements remain as true and as effective as ever.

> 1. Correctness of Diction. There is no more important element in the technique of rhetoric than the continual employment of the best possible word. Whatever part of speech it is it must in each case absolutely express the full meaning of the speaker. It will leave no room for alternatives . . .
>
> The unreflecting often imagine that the effects of oratory are produced by the use of long words. The error of this idea will appear from what has been written . . . All the speeches of great English rhetoricians—except when addressing highly cultured audiences—display an uniform preference for short, homely words of common usage—so long as such words can fully express their thoughts and feelings.

Selection of language is of paramount importance. When speaking, or writing, make sure each word is carefully selected to convey your exact meaning. Churchill notes too that flowery and verbose language actually detracts from attempts to communicate and persuade. The focus of communication should be what you are trying to convey—don't detract from that by muddling the message with complicated prose. Stick to the basics.

> 2. Rhythm. The great influence of sound on the human brain is well known. The sentences of the orator when he appeals to his art become long, rolling and sonorous. The peculiar balance of the phrases produces a cadence which resembles blank verse rather than prose. It would be easy to multiply examples since nearly every famous peroration in the English language might be quoted.

As Churchill notes, any famous text or quote that you know by heart likely flows along its own unique rhythm. Lyrical language is a lost art in most of the modern world.[1] But mastery of the establishment of rhythm in your speech and writing will lead to easier digestion by its audience. Alliteration, anaphora, and allusion should be part and parcel of your persuasive skills.

> 3. Accumulation of Argument. The climax of oratory is reached by a rapid succession of waves of sound and vivid pictures. The audience is delighted by the changing scenes presented to their imagination. Their ear is tickled by the rhythm of the language. The enthusiasm rises. A series of facts is brought forward all pointing in a common direction. The end appears in view before it is reached. The crowd anticipates the conclusion and the last words fall amid a thunder of assent.

You have to be headed somewhere—and your audience should pick up on it. You can't jump around when speaking, going from one disparate point to another. There needs to be an over-arching structure to your speech that your audience is able to follow. Effective communication builds like a crescendo in music, constantly growing and building upon itself, working its way to a grand finale. By the time the finale is

---

1. See Martin Luther King Jr.'s "I Have A Dream" speech for beautiful use of rhythm in modern times.

reached, it should be palpable to the audience. They know it is coming and are eager for the experience.

> 4. Analogy. The ambition of human beings to extend their knowledge favours the belief that the unknown is only an extension of the known: that the abstract and the concrete are ruled by similar principles: that the finite and the infinite are homogeneous. An apt analogy connects or appears to connect these distant spheres. It appeals to the everyday knowledge of the hearer and invites him to decide the problems that have baffled his powers of reason by the standard of the nursery and the heart.

A well-developed analogy—"an Iron Curtain"—can be more powerful than thousands of words. The most effective communicators are masters of analogy. A good analogy makes the foreign, familiar, and the clouded clear. A well-tuned analogy may win over a more technically sound argument because, while theoretically Logos (logic) should prevail, most people are more prone to be swayed by Pathos (emotional) appeal. People may forgo what is in their heads for what seems familiar in their hearts, if they can be drawn in by effective use of analogy.

> 5. Wild Extravagance. A tendency to wild extravagance of language—to extravagance so wild that reason recoils is evident in most perorations. The emotions of the speaker and the listeners are alike aroused and some expression must be found that will represent all they are feeling. This usually embodies in an extreme form the principles they are supporting. Thus Mr. Pitt wishing to eulogise the freedom possessed by Englishmen:

> > "The poorest man may in his cottage bid defiance to all the forces of the Crown. It may be frail; its roof may shake: the wind may blow through it; the storms may enter, the rain may enter–but the King of England cannot enter! All his forces dare not cross the threshold of the ruined tenement."

Churchill notes that such an appeal is best completed with a flourish of over-the-top imagery and outrageous symbolism, again appealing to Pathos instead of Logos or Ethos. In Churchill's example, Mr. Pitt notes that so strong is the rule of law and freedom in England that despite the disparity in prestige and power between a poor man and the King, both have equal rights and liberty in the eyes of the law. Such an extreme comparison hammers in the point about the power of the rule of law far more powerfully than a treatise on the topic might. A rhetorical flourish such as this at the right moment, right as the crescendo of communication is reached, can give dramatic effect and deep emotional appeal that will help bend thought and hearts to your cause.

PUBLIC SPEAKING

Being persuasive one-on-one is relatively easy. You only have to make a connection with a single person. But lawyers must also often speak in public. Even if you are not in a courtroom, it is likely you are going to have to speak in public to large numbers of people from time-to-time. Either at a bar event, a client event, or a holiday party—there are going to be times that you have to speak in public.

Many people fear public speaking. Most never have to face this fear. Yet this is not an option for lawyers. You must get over your fear of public speaking if you wish to find success as a lawyer. If you are unafraid of public speaking, that does not mean you are allowed to rest on your laurels. You should be looking for ways to practice your public speaking skills and find ways you can improve them.

Regardless, whether you are a novice or somewhat experienced public speaker, there are three disciplines you need to practice if you want to elevate your public speaking skills to the next level. In their book *The Articulate Attorney*,[1] Brian K. Johnson and Marsha Hunter provide a detailed overview of these disciplines and ways to master them.

1) CONTROL YOUR BODY

In speaking in public you need to look comfortable and confident. That means not fidgeting, constantly shifting your weight back and forth, or making furtive gestures with your arms. While Johnson and Hunter provide a detailed plan for controlling your body during public speaking, the two main points to follow are to maintain conscious control of your breathing as you begin and to have a ritual you follow before you engage in public speaking.

---

1. ISBN 978-0-9796895-9-8

Deep, deliberate breathing has a significant calming effect on the body. It's why people say, "Take a deep breath." Slowing your respiration slows your heart rate and helps release tension from your body. When your brain is spiraling out of control, knowing that you are about to stand up and speak in front of 100 people, the ability to have conscious control of at least one thing can help calm your nerves and your mind.

Johnson and Hunter also go into the benefits of having a ritual. Having prescribed behavior that you engage in before you speak in public can help put you in the right state of mind. Ritualized behavior is important to many top performers—not just in law, but in almost any type of performance. Most top athletes have set activities they engage in at every practice and every game—and they practice far more than they actually play. By engaging in ritualized behavior before practice, they are able to transfer that sort of calm readiness to their bodies when it is time to actually perform in a game.

Take time to develop a ritual that you engage in before you practice speaking in public. Practice it again and again until it becomes natural and unthinking. Then when it is time to speak in public, perform the ritual, and you are much more likely to calm your body and your mind.

2) CONTROL YOUR MIND

A ritual will not only help your body, but also your mind. It is often not enough. Quite frequently our minds get worked up before speaking in public no matter what we do. Before speaking in public, people will try and force themselves to calm down, frantically telling themselves to "relax." But Johnson and Hunter instead encourage you to get worked up and raise your energy level. Anxiety and anxiousness are methods your mind uses to prepare itself for activity. Embrace them. Let your mind raise its energy level and bring it to the fore.

When you begin to speak, let your pent up energy flow out as you begin speaking. Allow it to give your voice power and your words conviction. Nervous energy is not something to be bottled up or suppressed—instead, harness it, and make it a part of your public speaking.

Another aspect of public speaking that can make your mind go into overdrive and panic is fear of silence. But silence is a necessary part of public speaking. If you are always talking, then your audience never has time to digest what you are saying. As Johnson and Hunter note, "silence is punctuation." Become comfortable with pauses in your speaking. Use silence to shift gears and transfer between topics. Silence is not something to be feared but something to be embraced.

3) CONTROL YOUR VOICE

There are a number of tactics that Johnson and Hunter provide that can help with finding a steady rhythm for your voice when public speaking, but perhaps the most clever is simply to think of the *Pledge of Allegiance to the United States of America*. All children learn the *Pledge* and the cadence at which it is delivered. The *Pledge* proceeds at a deliberate pace, focusing on phrases, not sentences. Adopt the rhythm of the *Pledge* to your public speaking, and you should find yourself slowing down and speaking at a more refined pace that makes it easier for your audience to digest your material.

*****

If you can manage to follow these three disciplines, then you will increase your comfort and effectiveness in public speaking dramatically. If you feel the need for more in-depth strategies and tactics for speaking in public, I recommend you pick up *The Articulate Attorney*. It's an excellent resource that provides well-researched and tested methods for developing confidence in public speaking.

DRESS UP

Hopefully you can write and speak like a lawyer, but do you look like one? Law is one of the few professions in which a suit is required—at least if you are going to be in court. Even while just merely in the office, lawyers will often dress in suits. A suit is the uniform of a lawyer.

Yet in the past couple of decades, the suit has generally faded away from most of the business world. Business casual has become the norm. Ties have all but disappeared and suit jackets are often optional. There has been a general dressing down in the world of business.

But if you are going to be a lawyer, you need to dress up. You need to wear the uniform; set yourself apart from laypeople. You are a professional. Part of being a professional is looking like a professional. It is painfully obvious when people do not wear suits often. They are uncomfortable, pulling at their neck and shifting the shoulders around in their suit. You need to be comfortable in a suit.

You need to be comfortable in a suit because you need to project confidence to other people, and no one who is outwardly nervous or anxious will ever come across as confident. You need to be able to appear confident, especially in front of judges and opposing counsel, but also in front of clients, friends, and strangers. Your appearance communicates volumes about who you are. Recall earlier the laziness of our brains and how they revert into following pattern recognition when dealing with routine situations. This is especially true with the way we dress.

Our brains immediately categorize people based on their appearance. Someone in a car wash uniform = low status individual. Someone in a suit = high status individual. When you see someone in a suit, your mind automatically categorizes that person as carrying weight or authority. It's automatic, years of conditioning ingrained in you by culture and the media. As a new lawyer, you likely need that implied authority, as you are not going to be confident in your skills. A suit is a shield, albeit a cloth one, that can help ward off insecurities you may feel about yourself. But you have to be comfortable in it.

Of course, you have to be confident while not in a suit as well. You need the ability to be resolute no matter how you appear. But wearing a suit acts as a sort of ritual. Something you do every day before you go into the world. A way of putting on your game face before you hit the field. Eventually you won't need the suit. You'll accumulate the knowledge, wisdom, and confidence that comes with practicing law over a number of years, and it will exude from you effortlessly.

Yet even then, wear a suit. A priest has a collarino, a doctor a white coat—a lawyer has a suit. It lets people know who you are and what you are about. Wear it well; wear it with pride.

*****

Write well; speak well; dress well.[1] These are fundamental skills that every new lawyer needs to possess. But what about legal research? What about navigating office politics? What about the newest iToy? What about—it's not important. You need to focus on obtaining mastery over low level, basic skills. This will take a lifetime.

It is essential that you continue to develop these fundamental skills over your career, because the way you write, the way you talk, and the way you appear, all have a dramatic impact on whether people feel confident in placing their trust in you. Especially your clients.

---

1. Otherwise known as: thinking, communication, appearance.

PART THREE

CLIENTS AND CLIENT SERVICE

Law school teaches you how to think. It helps you learn the particular type of analytical reasoning necessary to be a lawyer. You learn how to read judicial opinions and make sense of obtuse statutes and figure out that the most important part of a law is usually buried in 512(B)(2)(d). The entire focus is on you. Upon graduation and Bar passage, many new lawyers are proud and confident of their newfound status as a member of the profession and ready to take on a central role in a law firm.

But lawyers are not the main focus of a law firm. Clients are. Clients are why lawyers exist. No clients = no lawyers. It's that simple.

Clients do not exist to provide you with a living. Clients are not there to be a source of billable hours. Clients are not a fact pattern. Clients are people or businesses with real, genuine problems. They are in need of help and are often desperate or up against a wall. Most clients would prefer not to have a lawyer. It may be surprising to you as a new lawyer, but most people and businesses are not especially fond of litigation. They are not fond of sitting through long meetings regarding the nuances of contract language. Nor do clients enjoy receiving bills for astronomical legal costs—which often seem like a gaping black hole.

Clients want solutions. In particular, clients want affordable, effective, and fast solutions to their legal problems. This is difficult to provide. As the saying goes: "Good/fast/cheap—pick two." But that does not mean that lawyers should shrug their shoulders and not try. And lawyers absolutely cannot just trudge along, doing things as they were done in the past.

The practice of law is particularly slow to change. Built on precedent, and reliant on government, the legal industry is behind the curve of many other industries. Project management, automation, and the use of computer technology to optimize and streamline tasks have been at work in the greater business world for decades. Yet practices and technologies to help improve efficiency and effectiveness in the legal industry have really only taken off in the 21st century. For a long time, the legal industry was a seller's market. Law firms dictated to clients their costs and procedures. But clients got smarter, technology improved, and law schools churned out too many lawyers.

The legal industry has become a buyer's market from the perspective of a client. There are plenty of law firms to choose from, competing on every aspect for the attention of potential clients. While slow to change in the past, many firms now embrace any sort of new technology or procedures that might help them compete with other law firms. But there is another reason that some lawyers have been resistant to change. *It is that they have their clients' best interests in mind.* It is a lawyer's job to envision what could go wrong. What disasters lay in wait with the embrace of new ideas and technology? What may seem like a good idea to a client may be a disaster from a legal or practical perspective.

So a good lawyer cultivates a culture of cynicism and learns to look for the negative side of all things. Many new lawyers complain that this eats away at them—that by regularly adopting an attitude of cynicism, it eventually creeps its way into their personal lives. This is why it is important to find some type of balance in your life. Not work-life balance, but an internal balance. One that allows you to address work problems with a work mindset, and your personal problems with a different one. This will take time, and you will slip up from time to time. Just be aware of it, take note, and try again next time. But remember, the practice of law is not about the lawyer, it is about the client. The client comes to a lawyer in a vulnerable state in need of help. The cost, the privilege, of being a lawyer is that you take their problems on as your own.

THE PRIVILEGE OF BEING A SERVANT

Being a lawyer is not a regular job. It is a profession. A unique role in our society. The only other professions that hold somewhat analogous roles are that of doctors and clergy. Doctors have patients, clergy have congregations, lawyers have clients. Many other businesses or jobs have clients, but not in the way that doctors, clergy, and lawyers do.

What sets doctors, clergy, and lawyers apart are their oaths: a promise calling upon something or someone sacred, usually God, to bind them to their word. While lawyers' oaths vary from state to state, each includes some variation of the following promises:

- To support the Constitution of their State and the United States
- To conduct themselves with truth and honor
- Respect clients, the courts, and its officers
- Maintain the confidences of their clients
- Abstain from bringing unjust actions
- To serve the cause of justice

It is not glamorous; it is a solemn vow of service. It is one of the great unknown truths to many who enter the profession. Being a lawyer is not a grand role, nor is it a central one. Lawyers are adjuncts. They exist in support of other people and causes.

I often think of lawyers as *samurai*, as in its original intent—"those who serve in close attendance to nobility." While it is unlikely that a lawyer will have nobility as clients, the role of a servant in close attendance strikes me as an apt one. That's what you are as a lawyer. A warrior who fights for others, those that cannot battle for themselves. It is not an exalted role. It is an inferior one. It is deliberately placing others' needs ahead of your own. Lowering yourself so you can allow others to rise up. You are not the master, you are the servant—and it is a privilege to be one.

It is our oaths that differentiate lawyers, doctors, and the clergy from other people. No banker swears to keep your secrets; no middle manager vows to uphold the truth.

Yes, the oaths we take are merely words, but it is our intent and actions that give them meaning. For some lawyers, their actions and intent make their oaths a lie. Given the general reputation of lawyers as a whole, people would likely assume lawyers take their oaths lightly. Lip service to a bygone time.

But to good lawyers—those who are successful in their practice, admired by their peers, and serve and inspire new generations of lawyers—their word is their most prized quality.

Yet these lawyers do not attract attention. They tend not to make headlines or be the butt of jokes at parties. And it is because they toil quietly. It is not about them or their office or their success and failure. For these good lawyers, their role is one of service.

Service to the client, service to the law, service to the court.

Everything else is secondary.

SHIFTING PERSPECTIVES

An easy and lazy habit that you can have as a lawyer is only seeing things from the perspective of a lawyer. Yes, you are trained to deconstruct problems and look for weakness. Yes, you approach situations with a cynical perspective. But that does not mean that it is the only perspective that you need to have.

One of the most voiced complaints of clients is that their lawyer doesn't understand their view or their perspective on a case or matter. This is likely due to a breakdown of communication between the lawyer and the client, and more than likely it is the lawyer's fault. As a lawyer, it is very easy to fall into entrenched patterns and lines of thought. So easy that it is often difficult to step back from your role as a lawyer, and look at a case or a problem as a layperson or client. Harvard professor Theodore Levitt most aptly summed up this concept with his famous observation: "People don't want to buy a quarter-inch drill. They want a quarter-inch hole!"

A lawyer is often apt to think of the law—the drill. How to use it, apply it, and make it work in any particular situation. But a client does not really care about the law; they care about the solution to their problem—the quarter-inch hole.

Clients do not care about the fine details or subtle nuances of case law or code sections. They are not concerned about the clever timing of your motion work or other "inside baseball" shop talk. All clients see are their problems—they are being sued, facing incarceration, in need of a prenuptial agreement. Your approach to these problems is largely inconsequential. What clients want are effective, efficient solutions to their problems. Whether to pursue litigation, draft a contract, or perhaps just make a phone call or write a letter, it is a lawyer's job to know which is needed and to explain it in terms the client can understand.

This is why it is important for lawyers to regularly spend time with people who are not lawyers. Once you become entrenched in the profession, it is very easy to spend time only with other lawyers, often to your detriment. Spending the majority of your time with only lawyers can skew and narrow your view. It can be easy to forget how people view the legal system and lawyers—as opaque and anachronistic. As such, it is necessary to regularly be in the presence of non-lawyers. Talk with them about things—the law, sports, anything at all.

Observe how people communicate, how they explain things. In particular, pay close attention to people you find captivating, people who grab your attention and keep it. Study people who can make complex topics seem simple. More often than not, these people are specialists in their field, having gone deep into a particular topic. Many times, people go so deep that they are unable to convey their deep understanding in a way that is accessible to the uninitiated.

But the people who do have specialized knowledge and can convey it in a way that is accessible to the uninformed have the ability to view their subject matter from a different perspective than that of an expert. They can step outside themselves and look at things as a beginner would or perhaps someone with only superficial knowledge of the field. And the truly skilled in communication can adapt their message to differing audiences. The people who can do this the best generally have a very broad base of experience and knowledge, in addition to a specialized knowledge of their field of study.

Can you set out how a springing power of attorney works in way that would be accessible and interesting to a group of high school students? Could you explain the difference between a contingent remainder and an executory interest using only cartoon characters? Being able to take your knowledge as an attorney and then convert it into something that can be easily understood by laypeople, and especially clients, is one of the most valuable skills you can develop.

A VALUABLE LESSON—RULE #1

The following story was told to me in law school by my Property professor, Richard Theibert. I present it from his perspective, as it was told to me.

*****

I had just graduated from New York University School of Law and gotten my first job as an attorney. This was in the late 70s. It was a much different time than it is now. But like most of you in this classroom now, I didn't know a damn thing. Just because I had a piece of paper that said I was a lawyer didn't mean anything.

So one day a partner comes into my office, hands me a file, and says, "Go to the Courthouse and handle this case." It was a DUI case. I wrap my head around the case as best I can and headed towards the courthouse—the location of which was about the only thing I did know. Of course, once I got in there, I didn't know where to go! That's how little I knew—I didn't even know where the courtroom was!

After a bit, I managed to find the courtroom, with my client waiting outside. Upset because I was late. We walked into the courtroom together. It was packed. Lawyers, clients, prosecutors, clerks, bailiffs. The judge had a full docket of cases that morning. Who was I supposed to talk to?? Should I talk to the clerk? Or the prosecutor? Or walk back and just knock on the judge's chambers? I didn't know!

Eventually I managed to find the prosecutor—who had about a dozen years of practice under his belt. We talked for maybe thirty seconds before he realized that I was wet behind the ears and didn't have any clue what I was doing. He told me not to worry and he would hold my hand through the process.

I take my client to the back of the courtroom and try to convince him that everything is going to be okay. Shortly thereafter, Judge Mitchell entered the courtroom. Judge Mitchell had an enormous reputation and was incredibly well-respected in the community. Being in front of him my first time in court made me even more nervous!

Judge Mitchell took the bench, got settled, and his clerk called out the first case on the docket: mine. I didn't even get to watch anyone else go first! My client and I trudge to the front of the courtroom. The prosecutor lays out the charges and proposed sentence, then I'm up. I get about a minute into my presentation of the facts when Judge Mitchell held up his hand.

"Mr. Theibert," Judge Mitchell said, with his chin in one hand, "Has Rule Number One been complied with?"

I froze. Rule Number One? What was Rule Number One? I don't remember that from Civil Procedure. Wait—we're in criminal court—what is the first rule in Criminal Procedure? I couldn't remember. Or did Judge Mitchell mean evidentiary rules? I managed to stammer out some nonsense while I wracked my brain.

"Mr. Theibert, approach the bench." I trudged up to the bench, trying to come up with an idea of what I was going to say. Judge Mitchell softly asked "Has Rule Number One been complied with?"

"Your Honor, I uh. . ." I began.

"Mr. Theibert, do you know what Rule Number One is?"

"No your honor," I replied quietly. I was embarrassed. Embarrassed to not know something as basic as the very first rule, embarrassed this was happening in a packed courtroom, embarrassed that I was going to have to go back and tell the partner what had happened. Judge Mitchell leaned over his bench, looked me dead in the eye, and very slowly said:

"Have. You. Been. Paid?"

I froze on the spot. I probably stood there for about five seconds before I managed to respond.

"Uh. . .no, your Honor," I said.

"Well then take your client outside and come back in once Rule Number One has been complied with."

I turned around to see almost all of the lawyers smiling to themselves. I gather my client and headed to the back of the courtroom. The client was flustered; worried that something had gone wrong.

"Well, what is Rule Number One?" the client asked as soon as we stepped outside the courtroom.

"Well," I said as levelly as I could manage, "the judge was wondering if I had been paid."

"Oh!"

The client and I spoke about it for a moment and discussed what the fee arrangement with the firm had been. The client had the money on him, pulled it right out of his jacket. $500 in an envelope. I took the money and we walked back inside and sat near the front. As soon as Judge Mitchell finished with the case he heard while we went outside, he called me up again.

"Ahh, Mr. Theibert. Has Rule Number One been complied with at this time?"

"Yes, your Honor," I said.

"Good, now where were we?"

I started back into why my client was not guilty. About a minute after I began, Judge Mitchell held up his hands.

"Save it, Mr. Theibert. Guilty. Next."

*****

For eighteen years now, every law student who has had Professor Theibert for a professor has benefited from his experience in learning the importance of being paid. I've done it poor service here; it really comes to life when Professor Theibert tells it. And that is the real valuable lesson of Rule Number One: you have to be able to tell a story.

If Professor Theibert had just said, "Make sure you get paid before you begin to work for your clients," and moved on, it likely would not have made much of an impact. But instead, he took an experience in his life—a humbling, unflattering experience—and used it to convey what he felt to be an important and significant point. Every lawyer who has heard the story remembers, both the story and the message.

No one wants to hear a dry dissertation of facts and law. Not a judge, not a jury, and especially not a client. Successful lawyers are storytellers, and that story telling begins when a client walks in the door. Hopefully, the client was referred to you by someone else. That is, someone else told the client a story about you. Then, your office and your appearance tell another story to the client. Finally, upon sitting down with the client, you have to evaluate their case and tell them a story as to why or why not you may be willing to represent them.

Simply put, stories are how people make sense of themselves and the world around them. If you are going to have clients, you need to be able to tell good ones.

WAL-MART EFFICIENCY WITH NEIMAN MARCUS FEEL

In 2011, Thomas Morgan, a law professor at George Washington University, said the following to the Florida Board of Governors and the Young Lawyers Division board at a joint meeting:

> [In the future] The lawyers who succeed will combine Wal-Mart Efficiency With Neiman Marcus Feel.[1]

The context of this quote was that in the wake of the upheaval in the general economy, and the law market specifically, lawyers are going to have to be lean and mean while still making sure it feels as though they are providing high quality service. Why? If it hasn't been clear up to this point, the legal industry is in a state of fundamental re-organization and change. Combine that with the current economic malaise and the rise of computers, globalization, and efficiency gains, there is more competition for legal services now than ever.

Outsourced legal services such as Axiom and Pangea3 are on the rise. They are able to provide services ranging from Regulatory/Compliance to Litigation at significantly reduced costs to corporations. Internet-based legal services such as LegalZoom, RocketLawyer, and others are emerging to provide low-cost legal services to individual consumers. Instead of going to a local lawyer for a will or incorporating a business, many individuals now feel confident in doing it themselves.

---

1. James Levy, *Prof Says Lawyers of Future Must Offer "Wal-Mart Efficiency with a Nieman Marcus Feel"*, LEGAL SKILLS PROF BLOG (Aug. 14, 2011), http://lawprofessors .typepad.com/legal_skills/2011/08/law-prof-says-lawyers-of-future-must-offer-wal -mart-efficiency-with-a-neiman-marcus-feel.html.

Combined they put more pressure on lawyers to deliver more efficient, lower-cost legal services than has ever existed. There is a constant drive to lower the bottom line and make things cheaper and faster. There is an increasing push for virtual practices, unbundled services, and automated document assembly.

RocketLawyer in particular drew much attention when Google invested $18.5 million in the company in 2011. The fact that Google saw this area as something that they wished to be involved in was seen as proof that Internet-based legal services were going to be a hotbed of growth in the 21st century. The purchase of RocketLawyer was lauded as the arrival of Internet-based legal services.

BUT WHAT ABOUT QUALITY?

When Google invested in RocketLawyer, it had many people talking about the cost-saving to clients or the efficiency of service or the convenience that these new services will provide. Everything centered on the low overhead that these companies are able to provide, cutting costs and passing along (some) of the savings to prospective clients—breathless discussion on how automation and computerization enables legal services companies to provide commoditized products that can be tweaked to fit many consumers' needs without the need of lawyers.

Somewhere in all of the excitement that this new technology provides—any mention of providing high quality, competent, experienced legal services to clients seems to have gone missing.

Convenience and cost-saving are to be lauded and sought after. Too long has the legal industry been able to coast by without any sort of push for efficiency in its products and services. But the practice of law is distinct from other businesses as well. At some point, the push for efficiency can become overwhelming and dangerous.

Lawyers are advocates. Yes, we should use technology to make ourselves more accessible to clients or to help streamline boilerplate work and services. But we are also here to step into other people's shoes and assume their problems as our own. That does not mean working through some documents at a break-neck pace, or letting a form generator create a contract that a lawyer gives a cursory review. It does not mean using "off-the-shelf" solutions for every problem or trying to have a template for everything that comes into the office.

Being a lawyer often means spending half an hour on crafting a one paragraph email to a client to make sure it is as clear and helpful as possible, while only billing .1 hours. It means churning out paper copies of a brief for proofreading eighteen times, and eating the copying costs. It means handling matters for clients with a phone call or a letter, and not charging the client a thing.

At some point it has to be about more than Wal-Mart efficiency and Neiman Marcus "feel."

It has to be about Neiman Marcus service.

QUALITY WORK DOES NOT MEAN QUALITY SERVICE

Consider the following example: You take your computer in to a new local computer repair shop to have it repaired. A week or two later, your neighbor, curious about whether she should also use this new computer repair shop asks, "Did they fix the computer?"

"I think so," you reply. "It seems to be running smoothly, so I guess they did a good job." Then your neighbor asks a second question: **"Did you get good service?"**

While the second question is certainly tied to the first question, it is also distinctly different. Fixing the computer is the service provided, but it does not constitute the customer service experience as a whole.

Consider another example: You sit down in a new fine dining establishment with a reputation for excellent food. You dine there and, while the food is excellent, your waiter is awful. Incorrect drink orders, rarely checking on your table, and general indifference to your dining experience.

The restaurant provided you a fine meal—but did they provide you with a good service?

LAWYERS FACE THE SAME PROBLEM

Quality of work matters. Law firms need to produce exceptional work product if they hope to succeed in today's cutthroat marketplace. Yet technical quality does not necessarily translate into service quality. Yes, a client might retain a firm to defend it from a lawsuit, and the technical quality of the defense is paramount. But nearly as important is the perception of that service from the client's perspective. Again, this goes back to developing the ability to look at a matter, not just from your position as the lawyer, but as a client.

Is your client well informed? Are they able to have their questions quickly and easily answered? Is the fee arrangement clear and understandable? Has there been advice on how to avoid similar situations in the future? A myriad of other questions and problems may present themselves to the client and it is the professional service firm's responsibility to anticipate, meet, and exceed any expectations or problems the client may have.

Responsive, visible, and frequent interaction with a client gives rise to a client developing confidence in a lawyer. Confidence in you as a lawyer begets confidence in the services you provide. But it is also important to be flexible in response to the needs of different clients. It is impossible to have one set response to client service with which to broadly paint all clients. In his excellent book, "Managing the Professional Firm," David H. Maister provides an example of how there can be a dissonance in the perception between quality work and service in the context of a law firm:

> One lawyer in a large firm relates the following anecdote: One of our competitors [in real estate transactions] makes it a common practice to get a copy of the deal into the hands of their client within twenty-four hours of the closing of the deal. We think we write better contracts with more protection for our clients, but there is no denying that their clients are impressed. We are told they have a better reputation for quality of service than we do.[1]

One firm believes it provides better technical service, but the other firm provides a level of service that is perceived as superior by clients. Why the disconnect? Simply put, there was a failure to manage a client's expectations at the very beginning of the engagement. A miscommunication about the level of service and diligence put forth by the firm. A failure by the firm to understand the client's needs and desires.

---

1. ISBN-10: 0684834316

A firm can't just provide sound technical work and hope for it to be enough. There must be a firm-wide, systemic level of commitment to providing quality service. It can't just rest in the hands of the attorneys. It needs to go from senior managing partner all the way down to file clerk and runner. Everyone in a firm must be cognizant that their actions are a part of the service the firm provides to clients. How to develop this level of service?

I feel as though the best shorthand answer to this question was provided by Alexis Ohanian, co-founder of popular social news website Reddit. After leaving Reddit, Ohanian went on to advise a company attempting to revolutionize the travel industry in the same way Ohanian did social news. There have always been travel websites such as Expedia, Orbitz, and the like. But in 2010, a new company named Hipmunk launched, with a very different approach to travel websites.

It introduced a really great interface for searching for flights and hotel travel—far better than what other websites have been doing—with a focus on the user experience. Big deal. Lots of people have built a better mouse trap; it's getting it in front of people that is the problem. Fortunately Ohanian knows a thing or two about building an audience (Reddit being one of the most popular websites in the world).

When asked how Hipmunk managed to generate so much buzz about its product so quickly, Ohanian gave a very simple answer.

It wasn't some ridiculous SEO scheme. It wasn't link-spamming blogs or some social media strategy. It was a very simple concept that most people fail at:

"We do everything like we give a damn."

Full stop. That's it.

ATTRACTING CLIENTS AND BUSINESS DEVELOPMENT

So how do you build your own buzz? Okay, you are willing to work hard and sacrifice for your clients—but you don't have any. Whether you are a solo practitioner or an associate at an AmLaw 100 firm, you have to have your own clients. Because if you do not have your own clients, your own book of business, you are disposable, or your options are severely limited.

Without clients you are reliant on someone else for income and job stability. Instead of relying on other people to draw in business, you need to attract business of your own. If you are a solo practitioner or in a small firm, this is of desperate importance. But it is important in a large firm as well. As stated earlier: no clients, no law firm. So the big question, one that almost all new lawyers struggle with, is: **How do you attract clients?**

At the most basic level, it means being willing to give without expecting anything in return. This is often difficult for many people. People, not just lawyers, expect quid pro quo for the things they do. But it is often especially true for lawyers, as their trade is knowledge. Lawyers have received specialized, narrow training in a field and they tend to want to closely guard this knowledge as it enables them to charge clients hundreds of dollars an hour in return for access and use of that knowledge. It can be anathema to attorneys to share information freely as it might somehow devalue their knowledge assets. So lawyers start to look at interactions as transactions. Speak on the phone with the client; bill .2 hours.

Problems arise when this begins to spill over into lawyers' personal lives. They begin to weigh and consider relationships. "I've been at the bar with Bob after work for awhile now, I probably could have billed another 1.2 hours if I had stayed at the office . . . was this really worth it? What am I getting out of this?"

Life is not a series of set exchanges. Building relationships and growing as a lawyer requires sacrifice and openness. You have to give in order to receive. Not everything you do is going to result in some sort of benefit to you. If you do live your life that way, expecting every interaction or exchange to somehow benefit you in some way, you're probably an asshole. If that's the case, you have larger problems this book can't help you with.

You need to be free with your time. Lend an ear or a shoulder to another lawyer or friend. Become someone that others can rely upon in their time of need. Don't ask for anything in return. Just be there.

It might not have a quantifiable return—it won't show up on the mid-month billing report. But it will make you far richer in the long run.

ESTABLISHING A PERSONAL NARRATIVE

The first step in putting yourself out there is knowing what you are about. You absolutely need to be able to present who you are to people in a simple, cohesive fashion.

> The more you know about your beverage, the better it tastes. That's why so many wineries put so much effort into wine tours and that's why you're much more likely to enjoy your bottle of pinot noir if it has been preceded by a short explanation from the sommelier of who the winemaker is, where they're from and what exactly they're doing. There's really no way of telling how or whether any particular part of the story affects the taste, but the simple telling of the story makes an enormous difference.[1]

The storyline behind higher-end products such as coffee and wine increases enjoyment of such products by consumers. Knowing the background and history of the products makes it more likely that the consumer will form an emotional attachment with the product, which will in turn lead the consumer to establishing a regular purchasing relationship with the product.

So if this is true for "high end" products like coffee and wine—is it true for "high-end" professional services like law, accounting, and financial management? Should new lawyers be establishing a personal narrative? Should they focus on their "branding?"

---

1. Felix Salmon, *The More You Know, the Better it Tastes*, REUTERS (July 6, 2010), http://blogs.reuters.com/felix-salmon/2010/07/06/the-more-you-know-the-better -it-tastes/

First off, you have a reputation, not a brand (more on this later). You are a person, not a company.

Think of a strong "personal narrative" as similar to an "elevator pitch"—summing up who you are and what you're about in sixty seconds or less. Are you comfortable with who and what you are? Do you know yourself well enough to look someone in the eye, take a stand, and say this is what I'm about without apologies? This is difficult for many people. Not wanting to alienate anyone, people mollify their voices, adopting vanilla opinions and language. But you cannot dither as a lawyer. The entire point is to take a position and defend it.

So if you are going to make connections with other people, you need to be confident in who you are and what you do. A lawyer who is able to quickly communicate his background and history to his co-workers and clients is one who is more likely to be able to quickly establish emotional attachments and relationships with his co-workers and clients. But these efforts must be genuine and not tied to some sort of return on investment. Relationships are not financial products to be assayed, measured, bought and sold. Yet they are some of the most valuable things we possess.

GREYBEARD ADVICE FOR SUCCESS AS A NEW LAWYER

Shortly after I passed the Bar, I attended a rather lengthy CLE geared to new/young lawyers. The presenters were all either judges or lawyers who had been practicing at least twenty years. While each presenter lectured on their specific topic, they also took a brief amount of time to discourse on how to "succeed" as a lawyer. Success is an ambiguous thing that carries different meanings for people. Yet these lawyers and judges, who most people would describe as successful, were nearly unanimous in their advice.

Among the presenters, there was some discussion of technology. That lawyers need to be comfortable with the online court system. They all remembered practicing before email and all agreed that it makes things much easier than having to always send letters in the mail. Most mentioned that it is nice to have the statutes and case law available on computers, instead of having to maintain a library of voluminous tomes. But all of these things were a sideshow. They were "nice" or "convenient" to have—but ultimately unnecessary.

Universally, there were two attributes every presenter mentioned, and a third mentioned roughly by half. The attribute that always took precedence, and was deemed to be the most important thing to be possessed by a lawyer, was **credibility**. Absolutely above-the-board, more important than anything else, top-shelf credibility was the most important trait listed by every judge and lawyer.

Have an appointment? Keep it. Say you are going to do something? Follow through. Going to be late to an appointment? Call ahead and keep everyone informed. And most importantly, never ever be untruthful with the court, another lawyer, your clients, anyone. Period.

At a close second, the other "must-have" listed was **relationships**. It is impossible to exist in a vacuum as a lawyer and expect any type of success. Go to the courthouse regularly. Don't have a reason to be there? Who cares. Go and meet with judges, meet their staff, the bailiffs, DAs, clerks, anyone and everyone in the building. Become a known quantity.

Go to your local bar, become involved. Volunteer for committees, sign up to chair one. Go out in your local community. Volunteer and interact with people who have no connection to the legal world. Meet people. Have fun. Give freely of yourself and your time, it will come back to you threefold.

The final thing mentioned by roughly half the presenters was passion. Passion is quite popular these days.[1] Lots of wannabe gurus and business coach types telling people to follow their "passion" and everything will work itself out. I thought it was very fitting that it came in last, if it all, among the judges and seasoned lawyers who spoke.

Passion is quite a nice thing to have and it certainly helps to have a driving determination in relation to your work. But it's not worth a damn if you're regarded as unethical and no one likes you. Credibility and relationships have to come first. Passion is important, but it is a secondary motivator. Something that comes after, or perhaps while you prove yourself to others. Treat your credibility as your most valuable asset, treat others better than you expect to be treated, and as your reputation and success grows, the passion part will work itself out.

---

1. An unfortunate trend. More on passion later in the book.

TELLING THEM WHAT THEY DON'T WANT TO HEAR

The underlying foundation of a client attorney relationship is trust. Without absolute trust, the relationship will decay. Clients are placing their trust in you to help them solve their problems; they cannot do it without you. This is a vulnerable position to be in. Most people like to think that they can take care of themselves and are self-reliant. It is only in dire circumstances that they need to rely on others to care for them. Doctors, clergy, and lawyers often fall into these roles. When people need medical advice, they turn to doctors. When they need spiritual guidance they turn to leaders in their faith. And when they have trouble with the law, they need an attorney.

In all of these situations, trust is of paramount importance because, at some point, it is likely the professional will be the bearer of bad news. Cases are not always going to go your way. A twenty-year-old will is not as clear as you thought it was. The contract the client agreed to has some clause that will trip up a deal. In situations such as these, you have to be able to tell the client the truth, and the client has to trust you in that moment, that you have read the law and facts correctly, and that you can steer them towards the best way to resolve the situation.

While clients may want to be friendly with you, you are not their friend. That is not the role a lawyer fills. You are their advocate. You are not a shoulder to cry on. Nor are you someone who is there to merely rubber stamp whatever decisions the client makes. A lawyer exists to advise, represent, and challenge their clients if need be. Yes, challenge.

Whether they are aware of it or not, clients don't need lawyers who are subservient yes-men. If you have clients who want you to just approve whatever course of action they think best, you need new clients. Lawyers are there to provide counsel to their clients. A lawyer's role is rarely composed of only being the bearer of good news and platitudes. Providing counsel can mean telling clients they may to have to change their plans, questioning the desired outcome of a problem, or even just telling them no.

Anyone can crack open a code book or look up a statute or a case, but all that provides is base knowledge, not the wisdom of what to do with that knowledge. It's one thing to use a saw to cut a tree limb, quite another thing to use a saw to amputate a human limb. The tool is the same; the knowledge of how to use it makes all the difference. A lawyer's knowledge of what to do in a given situation is what a client needs—even if it means telling them what they might not want to hear.

RELATIONSHIPS ARE THE CURRENCY OF BUSINESS

Clients can come from a number of sources. Maybe you take out ads in the local phonebook, bid on certain phrases in Google Adwords, have a fancy website, or someone just walks into your office because it was close to the courthouse. These clients are hit or miss at best. They might have a good case, in a field of law that you practice. But they are just as likely to be self-indulgent and have no basis for needing a lawyer.

The best clients come from your "network"—the people with whom you have relationships. Someone who already knows you, who knows your practice and trusts you, is likely to going to refer someone to you who fits your practice. Essentially, these potential clients will have been "pre-screened" by your network and are much more likely to have a viable case or problem, rather than wanting to sue the government because their brain is being scanned by weather balloons.

The wider and deeper your network, the more likely it is that you are going to be referred potential clients. It naturally follows that one of the most pressing questions new lawyers ask is: **how do I grow my network?**

1. **First and foremost, you have to be present.** You have to be in front of people. You have to go to events. Rotary club, art classes, wine tastings, Bar events, CLEs, luncheons, softball leagues, etc. Anything and everything you can think of, but get out from behind your computer. Making connections with people on social media doesn't count. A partner at a mid-size firm told me he always chides associates when he finds them eating in the kitchen/break area at the firm. Meeting a lot of new clients in the firm break area? Building relationships with

other people in the community while you're heating something up in the microwave? If you've got time to eat lunch away from your desk, you've likely got time to be eating lunch with someone else.

2. Being present is the first step, but it's not enough. **You have to be involved**. Offer to help. Volunteer to be on a committee, write a newsletter, speak at events, coach your kid's soccer team. Expect nothing in return. Make sure whatever you do, you treat it with the same respect and dedication that you do with your work. Volunteering to help is essentially displaying your work ethic to everyone involved. You can either be seen as someone who is doing the bare minimum, or you can be seen as the type of person who goes above and beyond when they are involved on a project. Bottom line: invest in a community, and the community will invest in you.

3. The good thing about being present and involved is that it will force you to interact with people you don't know. In case it isn't clear at this point, **growing your network will involve talking to lots of strangers**. If your response is "But I don't like mingling with new people/I'm not good in new situations"—shut up, put this book down, and come back in a few years when you're ready to be an adult. You don't want to interact with strangers? Who the hell are your clients going to be!?

4. **Be persistent**. Many people join a club, or some other sort of activity, attend a couple times, fumble around without any results, and write off ever trying to network. This is akin to trying to ride a bicycle one time, not being able to do it, and then swearing off bike riding forever. If you're not the outgoing type, it's unlikely that you're going to be establishing lasting bonds with people the first time you attend a wine tasting class. You have to be steadfast in your commitment to growing your network. As Edison said, "I have not failed. I've just found 10,000 ways that won't work." Keep going to classes, groups, and events. Over time, you will be able to build relationships with other people.

5. The number one thing that people fail at in networking, which leads them to think that networking is useless, is that **they never extend the relationship.** You would think it's a plainly simple thing to do, but the majority of people fail at it. As relationships are established, you will have to extend them outside of where the relationship originally began. You're never going to grow a relationship with a person at some cocktail hour with 100 other people there. Large social gatherings are

there for introductions—a chance to make the initial contact, trade business cards. Once you've made the contact, the onus is then on you to reach out to the other person.

In reaching out to someone on a higher level of prestige and experience, many people will do this with some sort of wimpy email or note that says, "Let's grab lunch sometime!" If the person you are trying to reach is busy and successful, you're likely to never hear back from them. Instead you need to send an email to them like this:

Hey [Name],

Great seeing you the other day at [event]. I really enjoyed speaking with you about [stuff you talked with them about]. I wanted to grab lunch and speak with you more about [stuff, or things tangentially related to it].

I'm available next week on [give a couple options here]. If that doesn't work for you, let me know what's convenient and I'll work around your schedule.

or

Hey [Name],

Hope you're having a great week. I spent some more time thinking about [issues the other person was having at work] at [event]. I had some ideas that I think may be able to help you out with [issues]. Let's grab lunch and we can go over them.

I'm available next week on [give a couple options here]. If that doesn't work for you, let me know what's convenient and I'll work around your schedule.

Both of the examples reference where you spoke, what you spoke about, set an agenda for extending the conversation, and provide dates to make it happen. All of which is much more likely to get a response than a bland "let's grab lunch sometime."

6. In building a successful network, **the follow-up is the most important part**. It's like the follow through of a baseball pitcher. Their movement doesn't cease just because the ball has left their hand. Once you've had lunch or coffee or a meeting, you have to follow-up with a handwritten note. Not an email, not a phone call. Go out and buy nice stationary—not with your firm logo on it. Handwrite the address on the envelope, don't use a label. Use an actual stamp, not office meter. Thank the other person for their time. Let them know you're available if they ever need anything.

Personally, I have had great success with the above plan. I've spoken with many other successful people—lawyers, doctors, MBAs—and they all follow the same plan to some degree. Quite frankly, it's nothing new. It's the same recipe for successful networking that people have been using for decades. But I guarantee you that someone is going to read this book, try the above plan, and get nowhere. Then I'll get angry emails saying that I'm a liar or don't know what I'm talking about.

The trick with the above plan is that your intentions must be genuine. The angry person is going to forget an essential part of step number 2, even though I'm writing it twice:

> Expect nothing in return. Make sure whatever you do,
> you treat it with the same respect and dedication that
> you do with your work.

You can network all day long, but if your mind is not in the right place, it's unlikely that it's going to get you anywhere.

DAN HULL'S 12 RULES OF CLIENT SERVICE

A final word on clients, albeit not my own. As many times as I have tried to get around them or think of something else, I always find myself coming back to Dan Hull's 12 Rules of Client Service.

Dan Hull is a founding partner of Hull McGuire and the author of the infamous legal blog: What About Clients?[1] At What About Clients, Hull waxes poetically about life, work, art, and on servicing clients as valued customers in law firms all over the world.

Eventually, Hull codified his model of client service into a "12-step" program for lawyers, professionals and executives. In Hull's own words:

> The rules are not perfect, and can be improved. But this model works—if you work at it. If you follow these rules by building a disciplined culture at your shop where they are enforced and kept alive, your clients and firm both benefit as you go along. You'll see repeat business. You'll make money.

The rules are annoyingly correct. Follow them and you will inevitably provide excellent service to your clients.

1. **Represent only clients you like.** As a threshold matter, you cannot deliver true service to a client unless you and your firm "like" your client and I mean like the client a lot. In the case of companies, "client" here means GCs, clients reps and individual client cultures—or the company's personality. Practicing

---

1. http://www.whataboutclients.com/

law the right way and with enthusiasm is hard enough. And as a lawyer, you owe some of the highest personal, professional and business duties imaginable to your clients. If you don't like him, her or it, you should chuck him, her or it—as soon as you ethically and practically can. You will not do good work very long for a client or customer you do not like.

2. **The client is the main event.** Rule Two is the obvious "yeah-of-course-our-firm-knows/does that!" rule that may get more lip service than actual delivery in all the details of our work for clients. My question for now is this: If client (or customer) "primacy" were really the organizing principle for everything we do, isn't that in our interest, too? Doesn't that mean that the work is better, law firm staff and attorneys are pulling in the same direction, morale is good, we spend less time and money on marketing, we keep good clients and we attract new ones?

   And if we really get it, are we really doing it?

3. **Make sure everyone in your firm knows the client is the main event.** Conveying what you are doing for clients above and beyond what other firms may offer, and how you will accomplish that, needs to be transmitted clearly to everyone in your firm: from the big picture—what does the law firm do, who are the clients, what do the clients do?—down to the smallest detail—in what city is the general counsel's office, who works with the GC on that project, does she like e-mails or phone calls for short-answer projects? One way to start this process with a new employee is by having her or him read a short, amusingly-written confidential "Practice Guide" (with almost no procedures or "rules") on the firm's overall goals, your firm's service vision, client descriptions and genuinely useful ways to work—before the first day of work. Everyone must know it's about clients.

4. **Deliver legal work that changes the way clients think about lawyers.** Rather than "under-promise/over-deliver", which is essentially job specific, why not change the way people think of lawyers generally and what they can expect from them generally? Get good clients—those clients you like and want—to keep coming back to you by communicating in all aspects of your work that you care deeply about your lawyering for them, you

want to serve their interests on an ongoing basis and that it's a privilege to be their lawyer. Show them you fit no lawyer mold.

Oh, yeah. One catch—and the hardest part: it's got to be true.

5. **Over-communicate: bombard, copy and confirm.** The notion of "bombarding" clients with paper and information does have obvious exceptions. For instance, you work with a GC who trusts you and wants you to leave her alone. She doesn't want you to copy her on every transmittal letter or e-mail. Fair enough. Just be 100% sure you know what she wants and doesn't want. But aside from that, this is a "can't miss" rule—and I am amazed that many good lawyers express surprise that my firm informs the client of everything at each step of the way, and copies our clients on everything.

6. **When you work, you are marketing.** Rule Six is more a truth to be kept in mind than a "rule." This is where the needs of clients and their lawyers come together. It's about value to both. But you can't forget this one. Keeping or not keeping in mind the germ of Rule Six—that "when you work, you are marketing"—is the difference between having a financially healthy practice and having to close your doors. For my money, "Rule Six" is the best single thing you could ever tell a lawyer starting out. And, hey, it's good for both clients and their firms.

7. **Know the client.** The client, it seems, actually wants you to know him, her or it. Take time out to learn the stock price, industry, day-to-day culture, players and overall goals of your client. Visit their offices and plants. Do it free of charge. I think associates in particular need to develop the habit of finding out about and keeping up with clients and their trials and tribulations in and out of the areas you are working in. Learn about your client—and keep learning about it. Devise a system to keep abreast.

8. **Think like the client—help control costs.** Ask an associate lawyer or paralegal what a "profit" is. You will get two kinds of answers. Both answers are "correct" but neither of them helps anyone in your firm think like the client. The answers will be something like this. (1) "A profit is money remaining after deducting costs from receipts." This is the correct young

transactional/tax lawyer answer. Or (2) "it's money left over at the end of the hunt." This is the correct fire-breathing young litigator answer.

The right answer?

A profit is a reward for being efficient. And until a lawyer, paralegal or staffer gets that, she or he will never know how a client—or a law firm partner—thinks.

9. **Be there for clients—24/7.** Get used to it. We attorneys, accountants and legions of other professionals with corporate clients—at big firms, boutiques or solos—are no longer royalty. In the future, "returning telephone calls promptly," "keeping your client informed" (like those two items should ever have been a big deal!), smartphones and having effective voice message and paging systems will not nearly be enough—if it ever was enough. Color all that barely adequate. In order for most of us to be competitive, we have to get into the habit of "being there"—that means both quality time and any time. Good clients deserve this.

10. **Be accurate, thorough and timely—but not perfect.** Perfectionism is the Great Destroyer of Great Young Associates. Don't go there. Don't be so stiff and scared you can't even turn anything in because you want it "perfect" and you keep asking other lawyers and courts for extensions. It's not school, and it's no longer about you. Think instead about Rule 8: Think Like The Client—and Help Control Costs. Balance efficiency with "being perfect," and err on the side of holding down costs. If a client or senior lawyer in your firm wants your work to be "perfect," and for you to charge for it, believe me, they will let you know.

11. **Treat each co-worker like he or she is your best client.** Clients love to form partnerships with law, accounting, consulting firms and service providers of all manner with genuinely functional workplaces. They love work communities where the professionals are demanding but love what they do and solve problems together as a team of happy, focused people who stretch—but respect—one another. It's fun for them to watch, and fun to watch them watch you. **Clients want to be part of that.** Watching the "well-oiled" team is an image which

sticks in the client mind. If a client can experience your people working together in that kind of focused but loose harmony, it's contagious. They will want more. It's that last string in the major chord of a truly joyous place to work and grow.

12. **Have fun.** American law is extremely varied, elastic and constantly presenting new practice areas—especially in the larger cities. It has something for everyone. I am convinced of this. Please keep the faith and keep looking until you find it. Put another way, don't quit before the miracle occurs. It's there, and it's all inside you, in front of you. Simple—but still hard. It's a privilege and joy to do what lawyers do when they do it right.

And it really **is** fun.

*****

Hull's Rules are correct. But as he notes, they are not perfect; they can be improved. You are free to adopt and adapt them as you see fit. Make them part of your practice or personal routine and see what works and what doesn't. Make them better. Or find your own rules for client service, what guides your interactions with your clients.

Just be prepared for whatever you decide to do to change. What guides you now will likely be different in five years. Even the fundamental rule of client service—the client comes first—will be different. Not that the rule has changed; you have changed. Your experience and knowledge now colors your understanding of the rule. The amassing of hundreds of interactions with clients, handling diverse matters, and the ups and downs of practice will season how you handle problems.

This aggregation of knowledge is one of the necessary first steps in becoming a good lawyer.

PART FOUR

PROFESSIONAL DEVELOPMENT

Professional Development. Essentially, how to become a good lawyer.

- Becoming a good lawyer does not require a top floor corner office or mahogany furniture.
- Becoming a good lawyer does not require wearing Prada.
- Becoming a good lawyer does not require a new BMW or Mercedes.
- Becoming a good lawyer does not require advertising or marketing or branding.
- Becoming a good lawyer does not revolve around Twitter, Facebook, Google+, or some other social media 2.0 bullshit.
- Becoming a good lawyer is not dependent on what type of iPhone/Android/Windows phone you have.

Becoming a good lawyer requires failure. It requires screwing up a motion and having to re-draft the entire thing. Three hours of research down the hole only to discover a new case that destroys your argument—then writing off that time from your billing and not charging the client because it's your fault. It's miscommunication between lawyer/client/opposing counsel/third-party counsel/doctor/court reporter throwing everyone's schedule out of whack.

It's six hours of round-trip travel in the car for a twenty minute hearing. Early mornings and late nights at the office. Hours away from your family and friends. Giving up some of your hobbies, projects, and pastimes. Giving up the things you want to do in order to help your clients.

It's a 100 little errors and cracks and slip-ups that come through your work when you first start out as a lawyer. You're learning the ropes. You can't anticipate exactly how things are going to go. You fall on your face again and again . . . all at the expense of your client. Your mistakes become their loss.

If you are fortunate to join a firm or go in-house, your failures likely never leave the office. They are purely internal. Your work is reviewed, scrutinized, edited, and improved. A partner sends it back, covered in red ink. There will be advice on how to handle matters. You have fellow associates with whom you can discuss issues and bounce ideas off of.

If you don't join a firm, it's going to be hard on your own. You will need mentors, colleagues, and friends. People that you can rely on. More than likely, if you are in a large market, there are three or four buildings downtown next to the Courthouse that are the typical "starter homes" of new solos and more established small firms. Generally speaking, most lawyers in these spaces are all willing to "pay it forward"—offer advice or lend an ear to a new young lawyer in need. You might even be able to find some lawyers to commiserate with online—though it is a distant second to having people to meet with in person.

Simply put, new lawyers need a support structure that allows them to fail, learn, and grow in order to develop into good lawyers.

Or at least that's what I think right now. What I think could, and probably will, change in the following years. The truth is, even though I wrote this book, I don't have some singular answer on what it takes to be a good lawyer. I know what I'm doing—following my gut and the advice of my mentors—and it seems to be working for me. But I'm still a new lawyer too, learning the ropes and making mistakes. We're all different. What works for me might not work for you. It's your responsibility to take the things from this book that you find effective and discard the rest.

Once that is done, all you can do is bear down, be prepared, communicate well, struggle with balance, seek feedback, learn from your mistakes, and **do everything like you give a damn**.

In many ways "experience" is merely an accumulation of our mistakes and what we learned from them. How we handle these mistakes is what determines our growth and improvement as lawyers—as human beings. But, you can also learn from the tribulations of others. Learn from this book, learn from other lawyers, learn from CLEs, judges, everything and everyone around you. Develop a voracious appetite for knowledge and learning and make a commitment to improving yourself as a lawyer, not just after you graduate law school, but as a lifetime goal for your career.

MASTERY IS A JOURNEY, NOT A DESTINATION

New lawyers often strive to obtain a goal of being among the best in their field of practice, or to have a perfect understanding of a set of Rules, or to achieve mastery of a given subject.

But find a great lawyer, one of the best ones in your city or practice area. Ask them when they became "the best" at what they do. When they achieved mastery and no longer worried about keeping abreast of their practice area or trial techniques or no longer kept up with industry news. You won't find one. Great lawyers become great lawyers because they dedicate themselves to **relentless improvement**. Never resting on their laurels or taking their skills or position for granted.

Dedicating oneself to relentless improvement is not an easy task. In modern culture, we expect to get things instantly and with very little effort. Want to know the state bird of Wisconsin? Google it. Want to see photos from your friend's vacation? Hop on Facebook. Want to know what's happening right now in Paris? Thumb Twitter on your phone. It's so tempting to let this ease-of-use suffuse itself into the rest of our lives.

Think back to law school. Nothing was instantaneous there. Law school requires tedious amount of reading and grueling amounts of study. Long hours in the library and creating boring, minuscule outlines. Dealing with gunner students and completely out-of-touch-with-reality law professors. All to get that JD. But the JD is not the goal of law school. The goal of law school is to get you to think like an attorney; understand case law, statutes, and precedent.[1] You put in the effort and got the JD, but the JD is only the ground floor. Getting the JD is the price you pay just to play the game.

---

1. Note: How to practice law not included.

Just because you have a law degree doesn't mean you are an expert. It doesn't guarantee you success, a six-figure job, or celebrity. It's just a signifier that you are ready to step onto the playing field. What follows is up to you. You are never going to be an expert, done-deal, time to put a full stop on learning. That's not what being an expert is about. It's about an ongoing dedication to developing expertise, evaluating best practices, and accumulation of knowledge and experience that allows you to differentiate yourself from your peers.

Therefore mastery is not an end goal to be achieved, but rather a process and mental state in which to try and envelop oneself. It will never be achieved, but that isn't the point. The point is the effort, drive, and goal. The constant pushing of oneself to do more than they think they can. To develop a growth mindset and let it permeate every aspect of your life.

PETER DRUCKER'S FOUR UNIVERSAL ENTREPRENEURIAL DISCIPLINES

You don't have to take my word for adopting a growth mindset when it comes to evaluating and adopting systems to help you develop into a highly functioning professional. Look no further than Peter Drucker. Unfortunately, more often than not, when I mention Peter Drucker to a group of law students or new lawyers, I am met with blank stares.

There might be no one else who has had as much influence on how corporations function than Drucker. His ideas, thoughts, and approaches to management theory and practice are some of the most remarked upon and followed in the world. Drucker worked with General Electric, Coca-Cola, Citicorp, IBM, and Intel. He consulted with notable business leaders such as GE's Jack Welch, Procter & Gamble's A.G. Lafley, Intel's Andy Grove, Edward Jones' John Bachmann, and Shoichiro Toyoda. I'd list all of his achievements and awards, like the fact that he has won more McKinsey Awards than any other person, but I have a page limit. The point being, everyone in the business world knows Drucker and his ideas. But as law schools seem to want to pretend that there is no intersection between business and law, there is no business education in law school.[1]

In an article for *Forbes*, Drucker outlined what he felt to be four universal entrepreneurial disciplines that all businesses need to adopt in order to succeed. They were:

---

1. A failing that needs to be addressed, but beyond the scope of this book.

1. Organized abandonment of products, services, processes, markets, distribution channels, etc. that are no longer an optimal allocation of resources.
2. Organize for systematic, continuing improvement.
3. Organize for systemic and continuous exploitation of successes.
4. Organize systemic innovation–create different and new techniques that make your successful products, services, etc. of today, obsolete.[2]

While Drucker is referring to the development of successful entrepreneurial traits for a business, these principals are just as easily applied to developing new clients or internal firm practices and procedures. These disciplines can apply to speaking, writing, research, or almost any other area of professional practice that needs to be constantly improved.

They can also apply to personal development: physical fitness, starting a new hobby, or shedding bad habits.

While you might find them straightforward, a closer examination of the language Drucker uses implies much more. Let's break them down:

1. Not "re-think," or "downgrade," or "re-allocate" but **abandon that which does not work well.** Cast it aside and never look back.
2. "Systematic, continuous improvement." Not going to a seminar or CLE once every few months, but **integrating personal/professional development into your everyday routine.**
3. When you have success, don't "build on it" or "synergize with it." And certainly don't bask in the glow of success. Instead exploit it–**manipulate any success to one's own advantage through any means necessary.**
4. Not improve your current products or business services–make them "obsolete." **Compete with and cannibalize your own success because if you don't, someone else will.**

---

2. "Peter Drucker, *Management's New Paradigms*, FORBES (Oct. 5, 1998, 12:00 A.M.), http://www.forbes.com/forbes/1998/1005/6207152a.html.

This is not a simple four-step plan to success. What Drucker lays out is difficult. Again, the language Drucker uses is telling—he labels them as "disciplines," not as guidelines or tips. A discipline is training that corrects, molds, or perfects one's faculties or character. It is a system one adopts in order improve oneself.

If you want to thrive as a new lawyer, develop as a professional, and advance your career, you have to adopt systems in your life that force you to grow and surround yourself with people who will challenge and motivate you.

TO SHARPEN IS TO DESTROY

I came to law school a bit later in life, when I was twenty-seven. I had fully intended to go to law school after graduating from college. But I knew I needed a buffer, and I wanted to know more about how law firms actually functioned. So after I graduated, I spent a year as a runner/project assistant/gopher at a firm with around 300 lawyers scattered across a few states.

After a year there, I knew I wanted to be a lawyer—but I also knew I didn't want to be a lawyer right then. All around me were friends and acquaintances moving on to different stages in their lives. But I just wasn't ready to commit to law school. I was young and needed time to explore and grow before I went to law school.[1] I just sort of looked at my life and realized the thing I enjoyed most was *Aikido*—a Japanese martial art I was training in at the time.

So I just said, "Screw it. I'm young and this will probably be my one and only chance to do something like this," and I moved to Canada to train as an *uchi deshi*[2] to a *shihan*[3] in the art for nearly a year.

It was crazy and awesome and painful and beautiful—one of the best and most difficult experiences in my life. It's the sort of thing that's hard to encapsulate in words. Sleeping in a storage closet under the stairs in the basement of the dojo on a thin mat.[4] Subsisting primarily on rice, vegetables and PB&Js (okay, and beer on occasion). Training five to eight hours a day, five to six days a week. Bleeding toes and cracked ribs. Scrubbing toilets and washing mats. Friendships gained and lost. Intense spiritual moments of training and camaraderie,

---

1. Something I think many potential law students should do. You're far better off getting some experience in the real world before committing to law school.
2. "inside student," one who lives inside the school & trains for a living.
3. "master"
4. Like Harry Potter but with less magic and more bruises.

intense times of loneliness and introspection. No TV, no movies, no cellphone. A computer with a bare 56k connection and stacks of books to occupy my free time. All my possessions in a suitcase.

When I was an *uchi-deshi*, there were special classes reserved for senior students called *kenshu*, which basically translates to "sword sharpening." During these classes, I would sit in *seiza*[5] for thirty minutes to an hour, listening to the instructor lecture on a multitude of topics. History, art, subtle points of techniques, themes, etc. If you haven't come from a culture where sitting in *seiza* for extended periods of time is the norm, it's very uncomfortable. Like tough to stand up afterwards, you can barely walk, uncomfortable.

After the lecture there would be an hour or so breakdown on one technique, perhaps one movement. A pivot or a shift of hips or moving into position against your partner. A single movement could be repeated hundreds of times. Occasionally I would be told the movement was correct. Mostly I would be told that the movement was wrong.

It was aggravating. It was boring. It was difficult. Deliberate, long, tiresome, and trying. After the tenth repetition of a movement I would grow bored. At the thirtieth, my mind started to wander. At the sixtieth I was barely concentrating. At the hundredth, my mind had become still and there was only the movement.

Also, as the *uchi deshi*, I was the dedicated partner of the instructor (i.e., all demonstrations by the instructor were done on me; I was the "training dummy.") Instructor needed to explain a fine point of a throw a dozen times? I took a dozen falls. Student needs to see it from a different angle? A half dozen more falls. Moving among the students as they begin to practice? I trailed behind the instructor, waiting to be thrown again and again. Somewhere around the fortieth time you've been thrown to the ground in under half an hour, you sort of become numb to it all.

When the class was done, I would be bruised mentally and physically. Tired of training, tired of sitting, tired of thinking. I often felt broken (sometimes literally) after class, lying on the slim mat that served as my bed. Beaten down and stripped away.

---

5. Japanese style sitting, feet folded underneath you.

But that's the point. To sharpen a sword—*kenshu*—to make it capable of cutting and piercing, it must be ground and filed. The metal on the blade must be removed—broken away—again and again before the edge is revealed, which is a point lost on most people. An edge is never "created" in a blade—it always exists. The potential to cut was always there. Sharpening a blade merely strips the excess away, revealing the edge within the metal.

It's been ten years since I was an *uchi deshi* (and seven years since I've trained in *Aikido* regularly), and I can explain, in exacting detail, the intricacies of almost every technique. I can explain why uniforms are worn left over right. I can discourse on *fuboku no oshie*[6] from memory. I can be thrown onto concrete and pop right back up. All of this is possible because I was broken down again and again. Instruction, examples, and demonstrations were plentiful. Praise was slim. I look back on it with fondness.

As you begin your career as a new lawyer, you are going to be looking for guidance, searching for mentors and those from whom you can learn. In seeking this guidance, it is a mistake to only seek out those who praise you. If you need praise go to your spouse or your parents. In transitioning into a practicing lawyer, you need someone who is going to point out your flaws, poke holes in your arguments, and shred your briefs: mentors and colleagues who criticize and challenge you.

If you are looking for help in developing who you are as a professional, as a person—seek out those that will grind you down and reveal the edge inside of you.

---

6. "the balance of a log in water"

SO GOOD THEY CAN'T IGNORE YOU

Before you can select mentors who challenge you, you have to choose to challenge yourself. Make the dedication to improvement and deep work. Choose **not** to follow your passion. I probably lost a third of you just then.

But I have to follow my passion! My teachers said to follow my passion! My guidance counselor said to follow my passion! Every airhead pop-star in the media says to follow my passion! Guess what? "Follow your passion" = Worst. Career advice. Ever.

Yet "follow your passion" is perhaps the most loudly trumpeted career advice given to anyone under thirty. "Follow your passion" and you'll find fulfilling careers, engaging co-workers, financial success, etc. There's an entire industry of banal lifestyle marketing gurus encouraging everyone to quit their jobs and pursue lifestyle careers. Have the courage to quit your job, follow your passion, and it will lead to great work!

Yet there is mounting evidence that "follow your passion" is inane at best. Instead, people should follow their work. At the forefront of this research is Dr. Cal Newport, who has made it his mission to decode underlying patterns of success, in all their nuanced glory, in an attempt to understand why some people lead successful, enjoyable, meaningful lives, while so many others do not.

Dr. Newport collected much of this research into his latest book, *So Good They Can't Ignore You: Why* Skills *Trump Passion in the Quest for* Work *You Love,* in which he points out that great work doesn't just require great courage, but also skills of great (and real) value. Meaning that you can't just be passionate about something and hope it works out, you have to develop sufficient skills in order to produce great work.

Newport gives the example of a woman who had a successful career in advertising and marketing. But inspired by moronic lifestyle gurus, she quit her job to follow her passion of practicing yoga. She spent $4,000 and took a 200 hour "instructor" course. For anyone who has obtained some degree of mastery in a complex skill set, the idea that 200 hours will propel you to the level of "instructor" is ludicrous. For example:

- As I mentioned earlier, I spent years training in Aikido. I easily spent 200 hours on practicing how to pivot, one of the most simple possible motions you can make with your body. Front foot planted, weight sinks down, back foot slides back and around in a 45 degree arc. I've spent an hour straight doing nothing but that motion again and again. Tens of thousands of repetitions. In comparison to my instructor, mine is utter crap. Maybe with another ten years of practice mine might be as good.
- After leaving Aikido I studied Brazilian Jiu-Jitsu (BJJ), a competitive grappling art. In practice, most people just want to "roll." That is, to actually competitively grapple until one person achieves a submission over the other person. It's more fun. More alive. And while rolling is absolutely necessary to achieve any degree of mastery in BJJ—repetitive, dedicated drilling is just as important. Other people would roll or just leave class early and myself and my main training partner would stay and just drill the same basic arm-bar submission a dozen times, switch roles, *ad nauseam*. The result? We both had the fastest, smoothest arm-bars.
- In becoming a lawyer, law schools want you to delve into complex theoretical legal hypotheticals that are favored by career-long academics. Law schools claim this makes you a good lawyer. But the relationship between the study of law and the practice of law is nebulous at best. I learned much, much more about the practice of law while working forty to fifty hours a week at a law firm while attending law school. The day-in, day-out drudgery that it can bring. Document review, hours on the phone, never ending emails, etc.

After obtaining my black belt, did I consider myself a master? When I received my JD and passed the Bar, did I consider myself an expert lawyer? Of course not. They're ridiculous propositions.

Traditionally, a black belt has only meant one thing: you were now considered a serious student. Everything before was playtime. Training wheels. Getting a black belt only signifies that you have mastered the basics and are ready to begin dedicated study. The same is true with a JD. **Having a JD doesn't indicate mastery of the law**. It's merely a signifier that you are ready to step onto the playing field. What follows is up to you.

And passion is probably not going to get you very far. As Newport notes:

> The downside of the passion mindset is that it strips away merit . . . launching a career that gives you control, creativity, and impact is easy . . . Career-capital theory disagrees. It tells us that great work doesn't just require great courage [to follow your passion], but also skill of great (and real) value. When [the woman] left her advertising career to start a yoga studio, not only did she discard the career capital acquired over many years in the marketing industry, but she transitioned into an unrelated field where she had almost no capital.
>
> The result? The woman texts: "'I'm at the food stamps office right now, waiting.' It's signed: 'Sent from my iPhone.'"

SO WHAT'S THE ALTERNATIVE?

Newport instead suggests a completely different mindset. Don't follow your passion; instead, focus on your work. Become dedicated to what you do. Delve into deliberate practice and work. Become a craftsman. Devote yourself to your practice or profession. As Newport notes, working from "finding your passion" asks what the world can do for you. **Working at being a craftsman instead asks what can you give to the world**. How to achieve this?

A quote from comedian Steve Martin captures what is needed to build a working life you love. In a 2007 interview with Charlie Rose, when asked what his advice was for aspiring entertainers, he said:

> Nobody ever takes note of [my advice], because it's not
> the answer they want to hear. What they want to hear
> is "Here's how you get an agent, here's how you write
> a script," . . . but I always say, "Be so good they can't
> ignore you."

To this end, Newport suggests four rules he and others have used to build their careers.

Rule #1: Don't Follow Your Passion. It's too much to go into here, but needless to say, "follow you passion" is bad advice for most people. In his work, Newport lays out three decades of research that has shown that the traits that make us happy with our work have little to do with our personality or so-called "passions."

Instead, follow your work. Find what you can really pour your time into as a lawyer and do that.

Rule #2: Be So Good They Can't Ignore You. Newport has developed a structure called "career capital theory," which is built around the idea that says to first build up rare and valuable skills and then use these skills as leverage to shape you career into something you love.

This is akin to a growth mindset and the relentless pursuit of mastery. You have to constantly want to improve your skills as a new lawyer—to the point that others turn to you for advice.

Rule #3: Turn Down a Promotion. Not that you should turn down a promotion per se, but the provocative statement is meant to point out that control is one of the most important things you can bargain for with your rare and valuable skills.

Don't just take something because it comes with a salary bump. Control over your schedule, clients, and work are just as important as money.

Rule #4: Think Small, Act Big. Newport spent a great deal of time following people with career-defining missions—often a source of great passion. He found that these people developed rare and valuable skills before they identified a powerful mission or passion.

This is backwards of what most new lawyers have heard for most of their lives. But it doesn't matter if you are passionate about technology copyright and trademarks but don't know anything about IP law or haven't taken the patent bar. Build your skills first and passion will naturally follow.

Follow these rules and you should find your way onto developing a career you can find satisfying and enjoyable for years to come.

THE PROFESSIONAL LIVES BEHIND THE SCENES AND PAYS THE PRICE

Imagine you are in the audience at a majestic Broadway play. The theater full, stage set, lighting dim. The curtains part and the play begins. Drama and tragedy unfold over the next two hours. The performance compels an ovation. Done with the play, you and your company depart for dinner.

You're in Las Vegas at the latest Ultimate Fighting Championship (UFC) event. It's time for the main event. The lights dim and the crowd roars. The two fighters enter the cage. The championship belt is on the line. The chain link door is locked shut and a grueling battle of wills commences. In the third round, the champion knocks out his opponent. You and your friends slowly make your way out of the arena, heading towards the Strip for a night of fun.

Both the actor and the fighter spend days and weeks for their brief time under the lights and scrutiny of the crowd. The actor memorizes positioning, recites lines, and studies the character role. The fighter drills techniques for years, physically conditions for months, and studies tape on opponents for hours. All for one night.

These performances cannot be conjured up out of thin air. They involve work, study, and sacrifice, all of which is lost on the audience. The days and hours of training and rehearsal are invisible to us. We never know of the anxiety and fear that goes into each time they step on the stage or into the cage. We don't know of the support structure surrounding the performance. The director, stagehands, and the conductor. The coaches, training partners, and doctors.

We see only the tip of the spear. We only see Nathan Lane. We only see Jon Jones.

It's no different for an attorney. The hours of toil behind the scenes to draft a contract, prepare a brief, or develop an argument are not seen by our audience—the clients. Clients only see the performance, the final act, the end result of the late nights at the office and time spent away from friends and family. The client sees the will, or the email, or an argument before the court.

And let's be clear, largely speaking: **They. Do. Not. Care.** Clients don't retain you so they can be concerned about your problems; they retained you so that you would be concerned about theirs.

For clients, what largely matters most is the end result. Embarrassing failure or triumphant victory—that is what matters to the client. If failure is the result, you didn't do enough. If victory is the result, it was too easy and you spent too much time on the matter. No matter how much or how little you do, it's possible that the client will find an aspect of your representation to criticize if you did not properly manage the relationship.

And regardless of the last result, you have to immediately go back to the grindstone again. Pick up the pen, turn on the computer, answer the phone. Check the email, empty the inbox on your desk, call your spouse. Review the bills, pay off invoices, worry if you're going to make it to the end of the month. But that's all there is at the end of the day: hard work. Embrace it. Make it your own. Not a reviled thing that drags you down, but a constant companion with you when you wake up in the morning.

The idea of embracing discipline as a companion always brings to mind Henry Rollins' essay *The Iron*. For those who don't know, Rollins is an author, speaker and former musician. Rollins was the front man for the iconic cult punk band Black Flag for years. Since then, he has appeared in numerous movies and television shows, campaigned for human rights, and become an acclaimed speaker. But long before Henry Rollins went on to become a cult icon, he was a skinny, unpopular high school nerd. In Rollins' own words, "I hated myself all the time."

It wasn't until a teacher took an interest in Rollins that he developed confidence in himself. The teacher put Rollins on a weight-training program to get Rollins in shape. While Rollins was on the program, the teacher sucker-punched Rollins in the hallway when he wasn't looking. The teacher said, "When [you can] take the punch we would know that we were getting somewhere." It took months of effort and plenty of shots to the gut, but eventually Rollins took a punch and laughed it off. He had changed:

> It took me years to fully appreciate the value of the lessons I have learned from the Iron. I used to think that it was my adversary, that I was trying to lift that which does not want to be lifted. I was wrong. When the Iron doesn't want to come off the mat, it's the kindest thing it can do for you. If it flew up and went through the ceiling, it wouldn't teach you anything. That's the way the Iron talks to you. It tells you that the material you work with is that which you will come to resemble. That which you work against will always work against you. . . .
>
> I used to fight the pain, but recently this became clear to me: pain is not my enemy; it is my call to greatness. But when dealing with the Iron, one must be careful to interpret the pain correctly. Most injuries involving the Iron come from ego. I once spent a few weeks lifting weight that my body wasn't ready for and spent a few months not picking up anything heavier than a fork. Try to lift what you're not prepared to and the Iron will teach you a little lesson in restraint and self-control. . . .
>
> The Iron never lies to you. You can walk outside and listen to all kinds of talk, get told that you're a god or a total bastard. The Iron will always kick you the real deal. The Iron is the great reference point, the all-knowing perspective giver. Always there like a beacon in the pitch black. I have found the Iron to be my greatest friend. It never freaks out on me, never runs. Friends may come and go. But two hundred pounds is always two hundred pounds.

While Rollins' essay is about weight training—it applies equally to any endeavor that requires constant attention, commitment, and discipline.

So embrace your work, make it your iron.

INSIDE THE PRISON, THERE IS A PRISON

Professor Clayton M. Christensen, Kim B. Clark Professor of Business Administration at Harvard Business School and author of *The Innovator's Dilemma*, poses the following questions to all of the graduates from his course:

> On the last day of class, I ask my students to turn those theoretical lenses on themselves, to find cogent answers to three questions:
>
> - First, how can I be sure that I'll be happy in my career?
> - Second, how can I be sure that my relationships with my spouse and my family become an enduring source of happiness?
> - Third, how can I be sure I'll stay out of jail?
>
> Though the last question sounds lighthearted, it's not. Two of the thirty-two people in my Rhodes scholar class spent time in jail. Jeff Skilling of Enron fame was a classmate of mine at HBS. These were good guys—but something in their lives sent them off in the wrong direction."[1]

Professor Christensen was writing in regards to business graduates, but his questions are equally valid for lawyers. The concept of work/life

---

1. Clayton Christensen, *How Will You Measure Your Life?*, HARV. B. REV. (July 2010), http://hbr.org/2010/07/how-will-you-measure-your-life/ar/pr.

balance gained a lot of traction in the early 2000s and largely attributed to the new generation of lawyers entering the profession. They wanted more than just a job—they wanted a life: time away from billables and headaches and instead having some modicum of time for family and friends.

Then came the Great Recession and the bloodletting of legal jobs from 2007 on. Work/life balance was largely put on hold. It went from being the darling of the legal press to something that was given lip service on page twelve.[2] Whereas firms used to have work/life balance initiatives—in which they touted culture and lifestyle like they were Silicon Valley start-ups—when the economy imploded things quickly reverted back to the old way of doing things. Firms made sure they were efficiently leveraged and not bloated. Associates were shed. The associates that missed the ax were put under new scrutiny, from partners and each other. Could they bill enough to justify their existence? Could they develop a book of business? Could they raise the firm's profile and prestige? Any thoughts of life balance went out the window. The lawyers that didn't make the cut were just looking for work—life had to take a backseat.

A total and complete devotion to work came back into the limelight. A total adherence to their career seemed necessary to provide for their family (and pay back those six figure student loans). Time became a commodity again. One that many preferred to spend on areas that seemed to provide immediate impact—like reaching bonus goals—as opposed to taking that time to cultivate that which provides a more long-term benefit in regards to growth and happiness. Trapped in their position, they toiled away, slaves to their perceived lot in life.

I once had an exchange with noted Texas criminal lawyer Mark Bennett. Bennett was speaking in general as to how employment can be a sucker's bet, how it drags on people who are there for the wrong reasons.

"You think that homeless guy is crazy?" Bennett said, "You should see how you look to him. At the very least, think about how to escape."

"Escape is a state of mind," I responded.

---

2. Note to young lawyers: that's a newspaper joke. Boring news went to the back of the paper.

Bennett replied:

> Inside the prison
> There is a prison
> Inside the person.
> —Peachtree Street poetry.

It can be easy for a lawyer to become caught in their work and the lucrative compensation that comes along with it. Which can, in turn, lead the lawyer to increasingly define his or her success—not by learning, growth, and achievement—but money and perceived power. Just as a business executive's career should not be defined by investments and dividends, neither should a lawyer's be defined by judgments and settlements. As should be clear at this point, contributing to the growth of yourself and those around you—your colleagues, your clients, your family—is ultimately more fulfilling.

Of course you have to fulfill the basic needs of your family first: clothing, food, shelter. But people actually need surprisingly little. You don't need a new car, a new iPhone, a new TV. So much of what people perceive as "needs" are actually "wants." It's also quite likely that people want the wrong things. People want the car or iPhone or TV because they think it will make them happy. They look at the narrative surrounding the products and want that narrative to become a part of their own lives.

But products don't lead to a happy career, or a fulfilling relationship with your family. You have to find your own answers to those questions. Don't let them be answered for you by an ad agency or a senior partner at a firm. If you don't have your own personal, genuine answers to the three questions, take some time for them. Don't answer them now. Look at your schedule, find a bit of free time and think about your answers. You might not be able to answer them right away, but think about what you need to do to be able to answer. Taking time to do so might seem inconvenient or unnecessary, but the return on this small investment could have profound impact on your career and family.

PERSONAL STRATEGIC PLANNING FOR NEW LAWYERS

> What, precisely, is going to make you special (or even more special) in the marketplace over the next few years? Would you like to develop a specialized expertise in a particular technical area, in certain types of transaction, in the problems of certain types of clients? You probably can develop cutting-edge expertise in any one of these, but not all of them simultaneously. The choice is yours. All the firm asks of you is that you focus and stretch; that you pick a career-building goal and work towards it.[1]

Very few new lawyers begin their career with a plan—largely to their detriment. It's not something that is ever addressed in law school, the need to have a plan for your career. In the current legal job environment, most new lawyers merely put their nose to the grindstone and churn out work fast and furiously whether within an organization or on their own. The concern for employment and a paycheck trumping almost every other thought or need. But as has been said many times—if you fail to plan, you plan to fail.

Toiling away like a cog in the machine does no one any good. Developing success as an associate is not merely meekly accepting whatever task is tossed along towards you, but instead seeking out interesting work and assignments. Picking an area of practice and pursuing it with

---

1. David Maister, Managing the Professional Service Firm (1997)

vigor. Learning about the clients and their business and industry far outside of the required bare minimum to complete your work. It is choosing a path of development and doing everything in your power to go down it. Discovering this path is not your managing partner's responsibility. It is yours.

This is just as true if you are on your own. If you are in a small firm in a rural area, you will likely need to be a generalist. But if you are going to be in a small firm in a metropolitan area, you are going to have to do something that makes you stand out from the crowd of other lawyers fighting for business. It is a client's (buyer's) market at this point in time, with firms desperate for clients' business. Many firms will attempt to compete on price. But as previously stated, competing on price is only setting up the client to leave you for someone else cheaper. You must compete on value: providing specialized quality services to the client that makes them feel as though they are getting a deal. You just have to discover what those specialized services are.

No one is going to be able to decide for you what shape your work takes. You have to develop yourself personally because that will in turn develop the firm as a whole. Again, Maister: "Developing a strategy is fundamentally a creative activity, not an analytical one. It's about finding new ways of doing things that provide an advantage over the competition."

By developing your own personal skills, you will in turn make the firm's services more valuable to clients. So I pose this question to you: Have you found a new way to do something lately or are you just following the herd?

ORGANIZE DISSENT

Alfred P. Sloan, Jr., famed chairman of General Motors in its heyday, has been attributed with saying the following at a top committee meeting: "Gentlemen, I take it we are all in complete agreement on the decision here." Everyone around the table nodded in assent. "Then I propose we postpone further discussion of this matter until our next meeting to give ourselves time to develop disagreement and perhaps gain some understanding of what the decision is all about."

If you are like many other young lawyers of today, you likely came up through an education system that encouraged teamwork and consensus building in which everyone's opinion and input were valuable: warm, encouraging environments that allowed students to discover who they are and develop their own meaning behind their education. Their minds were not something to discipline and develop, but rather soft sponges to hopefully absorb information through osmosis. There wasn't really a wrong answer; what mattered was how did you **feel** about the problem. Which is nice if you care about the feelings of children, but next to worthless in the practice of law.

Dissent is an essential ingredient in developing thoughts and ideas. Disagreement will present alternatives to the obvious solution, challenge the conventional thinking, and force careful consideration of one's position. Dissent is absolutely necessary in the successful practice of law. Actually, dissent is the foundation for the practice of law. If everything was kosher, and people did not disagree, then there would be no need for lawyers—we'd all be living in a wonderful land filled with rainbows and unicorns.

But as rainbows are fleeting, and unicorns non-existent, it is safe to assume that disagreement and conflict are very much a part of the world. While some people have the luxury of trying to ignore disagreements—**conflict is the canvas upon which a lawyer works**. Analysis, arguments, and criticism are the brushes and paint. A lawyer has to be comfortable with these tools and make them their own. Beyond that, you have to be willing to have these same instruments turned against you. Even if you aren't willing, you are going to confront them when you are up against another lawyer.

If your ideas, plans, arguments, briefs, and the like are unable to handle the internal disagreement within your own office, then how are they going to react when they hit the real world? Do you really want to tell your client that you didn't explore both sides of the issue in crafting your brief? You didn't try to poke holes in your own argument? That you didn't research the background of a clause to be included in a merger?

What is opposing counsel going to do to when you show up and are unprepared for scrutiny? Give you a nice rub down?

The bottom line is that unanimity is overrated.

Organize dissent. Nurture it. Develop it. Certainly there is a time when dissent is to be put aside and an argument, brief, or plan of action moves forward. But to move forward without ever having faced dissent within your own office is foolhardy.

FIVE BASIC
MISTAKES
TO AVOID IN
YOUR FIRST JOB
AT A FIRM

1. Rule #1. Also referred to by seasoned attorneys and judges as "key witness Mr. Green." Always make sure you get paid.

For someone at a firm, this means that when you begin to work on a project, make sure you get a billing code. Keep track of your time and bill accordingly. This seems like a simple thing, but many people are not familiar with the billing systems of law firms and law school doesn't actually do that much in the way of getting graduates prepared for it.

There are a variety of methods for doing this, ranging from complex automated software packages to the humble legal pad.[1] Just find what works for you, and make sure you are diligent in keeping your time. This is true even in matters that are flat fee arrangements. Why? Six months after you have resolved a matter for a client, they decide that your fee was too high and file a complaint with the ethics committee of the bar. Being able to pull out a database, or tracking list that shows all the work you undertook in the matter, will go a long way to diffusing their complaints.

If you are striking out on your own, this means that you need to understand accounting. Accounts receivable, income statements, balance sheets, statement of cash flows, etc. If none of those terms mean anything to you (and if you went from some sort of humanities in college and directly into law school it is unlikely that they do), you really

---

1. The legal pad being my preferred option.

need to put everything else on hold until you do. The practice of law is a profession, but a law firm is a business. If you're on your own you have to be able to do both.

Find a local college, community college, or library and reach out to them regarding their small business programs. They usually offer some good, cheap basic accounting seminars or classes for small businesses. Oftentimes, regions and municipalities will have small business outreach programs as well. You can likely also find programs that specifically target woman- and minority-owned businesses.

If you're really hard pressed and can't find anything like the above in your community, you can always go online, though this is the second best option. Why? As should be clear by now, meeting with people in real life is essential to growing your practice. You know who else is at small business accounting seminars? Other small business owners. Guess what small businesses often find themselves needing? Legal services.

2. Being unprepared. Always walk into another lawyer's office with a legal pad and pen.

There's nothing worse than walking into a lawyer's office unprepared. Having to step in and begin discussing a project and having to excuse yourself to get something on which to write, or worse, ask the attorney for something on which to write, makes you come across as inexperienced and amateurish. This is true whether you are in an opposing counsel's office or that of a senior lawyer at your firm.

Wait, I take that back. There is something worse than walking into a lawyer's office unprepared: walking into a lawyer's office unprepared—along with someone who is prepared. This is doubly true if you do so at your own firm. The senior lawyer is immediately going to look at you and the other associate and conclude that you are likely short lived at the firm.

3. Not knowing when the game is up. Always ask for a schedule or time frame for completion.

In a firm, sometimes lawyers don't have a time frame in mind, or only a vague one at best, when they ask you to undertake a project. Yet, when they do want the results of your project, they will want them immediately. Don't get caught with your pants down; press the attorney as much as you can for some sort of deadline. Then, under-promise and over-deliver. Say you'll get it done by then, but turn it in early.

The same is true if you are on your own. Courts will handle their own scheduling, you just need to make sure you abide by it. But you do need to be mindful of scheduling when it comes to deliverables for your clients. This gets back to managing expectations. If you're not the sort of person who is naturally organized, that needs to change immediately. Whether you adopt a scheduling system like Getting Things Done[2] or use a simple wall calendar, you need to be able to lay out all of your responsibilities and tasks in a way that you can be organized.

Some legal matters might only span a couple of weeks. Other can take years. Either way, organization will carry the day.

4. Picking the wrong road. Always try to get some guidance as to what form the end work product should take.

Sometimes lawyers might want a formal memo, but often times they just want a quick email detailing some issue. Or maybe they want a breakdown of the formatting codes from an insurance company, in which a spreadsheet might be a better option. Or maybe they tell you they want a general description of an issue, as they are just going to forward it to a client. Regardless, you need to know where you are going with the work product. Don't be in the position where you are halfway through a project and not have a clue if it's actually what the senior lawyer wanted.

The same is true if you're working directly with a client. If a client asks you about a legal concern, you don't always need to give them a detailed, 20 page brief on the issue. Communicate with the client and make sure you clearly understand what they are looking for. It will save you time and the client money.

5. Picking the right road, but choosing the wrong car. Find an internal sample or similar version of the project on which you are working.

Different firms will have different policies and procedures in how they handle certain memos, drafts, letters, etc. It's important that you conform to those policies and procedures as soon as possible. The easiest way to do this is just to find similar work product that has been done before. Look on the internal network server. If the firm doesn't have one, look in recent files. Best bet: find the most seasoned paralegal/legal assistant there and become friends immediately; they

---

2. http://www.davidco.com/

always know where everything is located. The projects given to new associates are generally boilerplate stuff—you're too green to be given real problems that require creative and unique solutions.

Yet if you're on your own, you don't have anyone in the office to turn to. This is yet another occasion that illustrates the importance of developing a wide and deep network of other attorneys you can rely on. If you are presented with a matter in which you are unsure of how to proceed, pick up the phone and call someone you know who has handled a similar matter before. Discuss it with them. Find out how they handled it.

What if you don't know anyone who has handled such a matter before? Reach out to your network or local bar and ask around until you find a lawyer that does. Then—*GASP*—cold call that lawyer and introduce yourself. It's really that easy. I've cold called at least a dozen lawyers asking about an issue or for advice on a topic. Every single one of them returned my call and spent at least thirty minutes speaking with me. Why? Experienced lawyers know the value of having a network, of "having a how can I help?" attitude and mindset.

If the matter is really too big and complex and you feel uncomfortable in handling it on your own—yet you want to learn about it—co-counsel with a competent attorney who handles such matters and split the fee. This is a regular practice among a large number of solos and small firms. Most lawyers will be happy to co-counsel with you and appreciate the phone call. Beyond helping provide competent representation to the client, you'll also build relationships with other lawyers.

NATURE LOADS THE GUN, BEHAVIOR PULLS THE TRIGGER

It's an old saying about the effect of nature v. nurture.

I first heard the above in regards to obesity, weight loss, and fitness. Some people claim that they are genetically predisposed to obesity. That may be true—nature might have loaded the genetic gun in their bodies to incline them towards obesity—but their behavior (diet, exercise) will dictate whether or not that gun is fired.

We're often placed in situations that are not ideal or in which we have no say-so. Bad family, bad economy, bad job. But these things don't determine who you are or what you are limited to. All of us have been dealt a hand in the game, but if you know anything about Poker, you should know that your hand is only a small part of the game.

When placed in a bad situation, there is no point in getting upset over it. That's not to say that you should not feel anger or frustration, but that holding on to such emotions is ultimately non-productive. A very small, select group of people can take anger and funnel it into creative energy. Most can't. Instead, when most people are angry they become insular and shortsighted. They focus on problems, not solutions.

Many recent law school graduates are complaining about the current job environment for lawyers—new or otherwise. Yes, it's a down economy. Yes, the legal profession is in a state of change. Yes, there are multiple downward forces on lawyers—globalization, outsourcing, contract lawyers.

But that's just nature loading the gun.

Your behavior as a new attorney will determine whether or not you succeed in this environment. Are you looking for a job? Mindlessly sending out resumes to hundreds of employers is not a solution. Looking for mentors and like-minded colleagues? Randomly accepting LinkedIn requests isn't going to lead to relationships. Trying to develop your skills as a lawyer? Attending the cheapest CLE (likely iPads for Lawyers) will not lead to a new skill set.

You have to have a roadmap, a guideline of where you want to go and what you want to get out of it. If you are merely waiting for opportunities to come to you, then you have chosen the path of least resistance. And paths without obstacles likely don't lead anywhere. Instead, make opportunities happen. Get out of your home; go to the courthouse—even if you have no reason to be there. Go to bar events; introduce yourself to strangers.

Put yourself out there, take risks, fail, and learn from them. Complaining about the current environment does you no good. Instead spend that energy on making yourself a better lawyer. Don't wait. Don't make excuses. Make your career what you want it to be.

YOU CAN'T WAIT UNTIL YOU'RE READY

Another common refrain from new lawyers when faced with a new task, client, or assignment is: "I'm not ready," or "I don't know if I can handle that." But you can't wait for the perfect time to begin, to be fully prepared, before you take on something new.

The author Steven Pressfield regularly writes about writing well.[1] As an accomplished author, he is certainly entitled to do so. In conjunction with discussing writing well, Pressfield also often writes on what he describes as "Resistance." To Pressfield, Resistance is that inner voice we all have that tells us we're not good enough, that we are going to fail, that we'll blow it, that we don't actually want these good things anyway.

This internal voice, this Resistance, if listened to, will prevent you from starting many things. I'll call that lawyer I want to make contact with once I figure out something we have in common. I'll start a legal blog to help get my name out there, but only when I know enough about blogging platforms. I'll attend a community event once I learn enough about it. But I'm just not ready yet.

Pressfield once described a battle in which German Field Marshal Erwin Rommel, "the Desert Fox," discarded the orders of his superiors to wait until he was ready.

> In February of 1941, Rommel was given command of the brand-new Afrika Korps and sent from Europe to Libya, with orders to hold back the British, who had defeated Germany's Axis allies, the Italians, and

---

1. Though generally known for "The Legend of Bagger Vance," Pressfield often writes on war and military history.

had pushed them back a thousand miles to the gates of Tripoli. Rommel landed with less than half of his tanks and men. He had strict orders from the high command to take no aggressive action. His superiors wanted him to wait till all his forces had landed and the Afrika Korps was at full strength.

Instead Rommel hopped into his Fieseler Storch scout plane and flew east to take a peek at the British lines. What he saw, amazed him. The Brits had pulled back; their defenses were thin to nonexistent.

Rommel attacked. He had only a handful of tanks and virtually no fuel. But the audacity of his assault rocked the British so hard, they wheeled and withdrew. One of the quirks of warfare in the desert, where there are no natural defensive barriers like rivers or mountain ranges, is that, once one side gets the other on the run, that "run" can go on for a long time. In this case it was a thousand miles, all because Rommel started before he was ready.[2]

While Mr. Pressfield's advice is in regards to writing, it is true for any difficult endeavor: Putting off studying for the bar until you are ready, delaying the research for a brief until you are ready, deferring to write that Rule 50(a) until you are ready. Not going to networking events because you are an introvert, not submitting an article because of the research involved, not calling another lawyer because you're not ready for confrontation.

You are always going to be able to find reasons to delay: To put things off and find a reason to start tomorrow. To never believe in yourself, or ever think you're good enough. There are more experienced lawyers. There are better-trained lawyers. Lawyers who went to better schools than you did. Lawyers with nicer offices and staff and resources that you do not have.

Other people are going to tell you these things too. People are going to say that you're not ready or you're not good enough to start

---

2. *Steven Pressfield, Start Before You're Ready*, STEVEN PRESSFIELD ONLINE (July, 7 2010), http://www.stevenpressfield.com/2010/07/start-before-youre-ready/.

your own law practice or to lateral into a bigger firm. Stay where you are, don't rock the boat. Other people will tell you that the economy is too bad, that there are no jobs out there. You will be told that all the good clients are taken and there is nothing left for new lawyers. You'll hear people complaining that the legal profession as a whole is a scam and that there is no point in trying. The only thing you should do is get out—find another line of work and leave the law behind.

People like this constantly find ways to procrastinate and reschedule doing that which they know needs doing—until they are ready. Yet these people aren't ready. They likely never will be. They want you to be not ready as well. They want you to stay with them, be pulled down to their level. When you make the jump—when you're not ready—it causes them to doubt themselves. It forces them to look at their own circumstances and deficiencies. And they will resent you for it.

Yet you can't let your inner voice or outside criticism hold you back. There will never be a perfect time or circumstance when everything is in the right place. At some point you just have to dive in and figure it out. That's why you went to law school. That was the point. To train you how to look at complex problems, deconstruct them, and find solutions. If you can't manage to take the time and energy to solve your own problems—employment, getting clients, learning a new practice—you're unlikely to ever do a good job in solving the problems of your clients.

That's not to say that you should recklessly charge into matters completely unprepared. Don't take on a $100 million merger one month out of law school. But rather you need to recognize that lawyers say that they "practice" for a reason. Practice is "repeated performance or systematic exercise for the purpose of acquiring skill or proficiency."[3] Lawyers are never perfectly ready for what they do. They practice at it. They work at it until they get better.

"Ready" then, is not some perfectly prepared gameplan, set of skills, or resources at hand, but rather a mindset—a willingness to take on challenges and make the most of it.

---

3. http://dictionary.reference.com/browse/practice

MAKING PLANS AND CHANGING HABITS

"We are what we repeatedly do. Excellence, then, is not an act, but a habit."
　　—Aristotle, Nicomachean Ethics, Book 2

Developing a plan and sticking to it is easier said than done. Take New Year's resolutions. Every year people make resolutions; usually that they will dedicate themselves to some sort of change. People say they want to change their appearance, their friends, their family, their job. So, goals are set. Motivation is high; intentions are strong and good. Everyone likes to make resolutions, but few actually like to keep them.

Time passes. January gives way to February, then to March. The desire and intent behind the resolution is ground down. The resolution takes a back seat to the routine. Relationships turn sour. Work becomes pressing. The economy more dire. New habits waver. The diet slowly fades. The new running shoes sit in the closet, dry dirt cracked on the floor. Paper piled high on the desk, no order to be seen. The same argument comes up again between spouses—both respond in the same, usual way. *Why???*

Our brains are lazy. They optimize information processing so that as little work has to be done as possible. People constantly develop what is called schema (an organized pattern of thought or behavior) in order to interpret the world around them and provide a framework for incorporating new information. Some typical schemata:

- **Stereotypes.** "People from the South of the United States are rednecks—racist and poor."
- **Social Roles.** "Men should be the breadwinners of the family."

- **Worldviews.** "Libertarians are free-market wackos that want to eliminate all government."
- **Scripts.** "I've been working hard all week so I deserve a drink, or three."

The final one, *scripts*, is usually the root cause of why people fail at keeping their resolutions. How about a few more scripts, this time related to lawyers?

- "I have a JD from <insert prestigious university>. I will absolutely get a job upon graduation."
- "I am more valuable if I am 'busy.'"
- "I'd work on developing more business—if I had the time."

People have numerous scripts that they follow every day, largely unbeknownst to them. Deviating from these scripts is difficult. Your mind wants to follow the set plan, the old habits, the routine. Breaking a plan, deviating from the routine, and developing new habits are incredibly difficult for most people.

People tend to use a New Year as an opportunity for new beginnings in their relationships with other people and things. It's a set marker—something different from the routine. Tying a resolution to the New Year feels like a reset or a do-over. The reality is that the New Year—a number on a calendar—is an arbitrary thing, without meaning or purpose other than that which you give it. In the end, it's just another day, a notch on the wall. The only reason the New Year has any sort of meaning is because people give it meaning. Yet again, **why** do people choose the New Year to make resolutions? **Why** is it that when people say they are going to start a diet, they wait to do it on a Monday? In deciding to attend networking events, **why** do people decide to start the following month?

Whether people realize it or not (they likely don't), it is because they are trying to develop a new routine and they feel as though their routines are tied to a calendar. On some level it's understandable—so much of a person's life is defined by a calendar: school days, weekends, holidays, and the like all have a general effect on people's routines. More specifically, people have to adhere to their work schedule, significant events in their personal lives (birthdays, etc.), and paying bills.

For a professional like a lawyer, it's easy to become even more defined by calendars: docket call on a certain date, expert witnesses must be declared six months before trial, respond to client email by 4 p.m.

So in deciding to develop and implement a new plan, get a new job, meet new potential clients, or explore a practice area, lawyers tend to want to tie it to a schedule. So they pick a day on the calendar—usually the farther out the better. But many lawyers fail at implementing new plans again and again—just as do most people who make New Year's Resolutions. **Why?** Most people never move past the big picture stage. A grand plan is set: "Lose weight." "Get clients." But then there is no actionable plan set in place afterwards. In order to develop plans that you can stick to, you have to get granular. Dive down to the smallest of decisions and choices you make day-in day-out.

In order to effect change, you need to learn to recognize habits and patterns in your daily life. Because if you don't, it is likely that you will remain a slave to them. You brain finds it far easier to keep the same routine.

Get to work first thing in the morning: get coffee, boot up computer, read news websites, check email personal, check email business, look over work from yesterday. There went forty-five minutes.

Have some free time in the afternoon? Click over to Facebook or Twitter. Go smoke a cigarette. Check your brackets for March Madness. There went fifteen minutes.

Sound familiar? Your habits might not exactly fall in line with the above, but I guarantee you that you have set habits and routines that you follow every single day. In order to effect change, you need to learn to recognize habits and patterns in your daily life. Then, once you have identified these habits and routines, displace them with new ones, one-by-one, starting very small.

THE STRUCTURE OF A HABIT

Habits tend to follow a basic structure that you can learn to recognize very quickly:

Prompt—Activity—Reward

Prompt. Habits are generally triggered by something, a prompt. Think about the Russian physiologist Ivan Petrovich Pavlov and his famous dogs. Pavlov developed the concept of conditioned reflex through his study of dogs and their behavior. Specifically, Pavlov began ringing a bell when he would present food to dogs before they were fed. Initially, the dogs would only salivate when the food is presented. But after repeating the process a number of times, the dog will eventually come to associate the ringing of the bell with the food and salivate upon the ringing of the bell. People are no different. We tend to associate certain activities with certain prompts.

Time
- Most people tie habits to time—hence focusing on a calendar when trying to start a new activity. 3 p.m.? Time for an afternoon snack.

Location
- Where you are has a big effect on routine. Your environment has a tremendous amount of influence on what activities you follow. It's why many people fail at having a home office. They fall into the usual routines they have at home. (It's also why you went to the library to study when you were in law school.)

Emotion
- Many habits are tied to an emotional state. A certain feeling can trigger a response. Feeling sad; eat chocolate.

People

- People have set habits that they develop with people over years. If the only thing you ever did with a college buddy was go out drinking, and he comes into town for the weekend—you're likely going to go out drinking.

Activities

- Other activities can trigger habits as well. How often have you heard: "I only smoke when I'm drinking."

The first step in recognizing habits is to recognize the prompt that sets the habit in motion. The next step is to look at the activity that follows the prompt.

Activity. An activity can be anything. Checking email. Goofing around on the Internet. Biting your nails. Reading the news. Not doing anything (shutting down). It the immediate actions you take in response to a prompt that results in a reward.

Reward. The activity that is undertaken usually results in a reward. A reward can take a variety of states—sometimes physical, sometimes emotional. Hanging out in the break room might reward you with social interaction. Smoking a cigarette helps calm your nicotine addiction. Keeping up with the news might give you the feeling of being more "informed" than other people.

*****

Once you've come to recognize the structure of a habit, Prompt—Activity—Reward, you can begin to identify habits in your life that you want to limit, modify, or replace.

Let's create a lawyer—Jane Billsalot. Jane is a second year associate at a mid-size firm (about eighty lawyers) in Portland, Oregon. Jane has largely been practicing in the Intellectual Property group. Being in the Northwest, there is a lot of high tech work to go around that needs IP lawyers. Jane enjoys IP, but has mostly been stuck defending trade dress in litigation. Jane would rather work on the start-up side of IP—helping new companies with obtaining copyright, trademarks, and patents for their products and services. But she doesn't have much experience in that area, and she isn't sure where to start.

Regardless, Jane tells herself that is her goal for the year—develop expertise in a niche practice area. When she has some free time, she'll do some research on the topic. Or reach out to a classmate who does that work in Seattle. Or find a CLE to attend on the topic. Or some other thing that she says she is going to do but then never does.

Instead, Jane needs to make a commitment to setting small, specific, incremental goals that build on one another over time. The first step is to recognize that she needs to set aside some time to figure out what the hell she really means in the first place. That means freeing time up in her day to set aside for her professional development goals. But Jane ends up telling herself she is too busy. She has too many commitments and too much work to do.

Jane also loves hiking and skiing. She'll spend time in the morning hitting up some ski websites that list the latest sales on ski deals. During the season, she checks on the slopes for the conditions too—probably a couple times a day. Jane also chats over instant message with her friends about skiing, which peak they want to hit, who is going to make it out this weekend. All in all, she likely spends the first fifteen to twenty minutes of every work day this way. It all takes place in the morning, with her first cup of coffee. It's her routine. But it doesn't have to be.

If Jane is serious about learning more about a new practice area, she is likely going to have to make some sacrifices. With a full schedule, something is going to have to be cut out. Not entirely erased, but modified. Let's break down Jane's routine to see what we can find out about why she follows it.

Prompts. Jane is in the office, at her desk. It's first thing in the morning. She is drinking coffee.

Activities. Generally she is spending time online. Specifically, Jane chats with friends, looks into ski conditions, and checks for reviews.

Rewards. Jane receives social interaction with her friends. She also builds anticipation in looking at slope conditions. When hitting ski sales sites, she gets hit with a dopamine rush waiting for the page to load, on the chance that there might be a good deal on some new gear.[1]

---

1. Dopamine, a monoamine neurotransmitter and hormone, plays a major role in the brain system that is responsible for reward-driven learning. Every type of reward that has been studied increases the level of dopamine transmission in the brain. "Dopamine," WIKIPEDIA, THE FREE ENCYCLOPEDIA, http://en.wikipedia.org/w/index.php?title=Dopamine&oldid=555176003 (accessed May 16, 2013).

Jane doesn't need to erase this habit—it's certainly not a bad one. It's a positive social outlet and relates to her favorite pastime. Besides, trying to completely erase it and replace it with something else is attempting to go from one to a ten on a one-to-ten scale. Like trying to do an Arabian Double Front Flip on the first day of gymnastics class. Which is not what happens at all on the first day of a gymnastics class. Instead, people are introduced to basic tumbling, how to fall down safely. In gymnastics, you will fall down a lot. Rather similar to starting a new habit.

So instead of Jane making some wild commitment, like never checking about ski information or chatting with her friends ever again, she should instead commit to taking one morning a week to learning more about a new practice area. Jane recognizes that she needs to change one of the prompts in order to knock her out of her routine. So starting on Wednesday, and every Wednesday thereafter, before getting coffee, she gets a glass of water. That's it. Many of you right now are thinking that this is a ridiculous thing to do. But it works. One small change in the routine establishes a platform for future changes.

Jane now has water at her side instead of coffee. She knows she has water because she made the decision to have water instead of coffee in order to change one small part of her routine. That makes her think of her morning ski routine. She knows she needs to instead have a professional development routine. What steps does she need to make that routine happen? Suddenly, instead of surfing ski shops online, Jane is brainstorming on how to learn more about the area of law in which she wants to practice.

Eventually, depending on need, one day may no longer be enough. Instead, Jane might need to start with water two days a week instead. Or perhaps changing to water isn't a different enough prompt. Maybe Jane needs to have water and sit on the opposite side of her desk. Something, anything, to break the routine of what she does day-in, day-out. The point being, Jane only needs to change one small part of her routine to result in big changes.

The take away is simple: make plans, but change habits.

Don't get caught up in trying to make huge sweeping changes in your schedule to make room for finding a new job, networking with potential clients, learning about a new practice area, or anything else you want to change in your professional (or personal) life. Instead, study your personal scripts. Find time-wasting routines and habits throughout your day. Target them, and then make small, incremental changes. You will get results far better than if all you have is a nebulous goal of "improving yourself."

ADDRESS INCONGRUITIES

Law firms are bastions of doing things "the way they've always been done." Change is often not welcome within the legal field. See the continuous stream of complaints about legal writing [Hereunto, wherefore, premises considered, three (3) forms. . .] as an example. If you're a round peg, you're going to be hammered into a square hole whether you like it or not.

The same can be true for the manner in which matters are handled within your firm. Perhaps there is a set process for handling a routine matter—something that was put in place ten years ago and does not take advantage of modern workflow procedures. Coming in with a fresh set of eyes and understanding of computers and technology, perhaps you see a way in which to improve and build on it.

Or you're out on your own. You're struggling, but making it. You network with some other new young lawyers. You've got a few clients. Maybe found a mentor. Someone shows you how to file a certain motion, or they give you a contract for a certain type of real estate deal that they've done before. You look over the contract and find some arcane phrasing and a seemingly unnecessary clause.

You see the incongruities and think you can fix them.

Stop. No you don't.

Policies and procedures that are in place are likely there for a purpose—a senior attorney has set it up that way for a reason. The same is true with the contract. More than likely there is something there you don't see. Something their experience and perspective provides that you can't perceive. They are not looking at it on an individual basis, but how the process has been handled over the course of dozens of cases. The process is designed to address multiple problems that could occur along the way.

What might seem inefficient to you could actually be the appropriate amount of due diligence required to make sure something is done right.

For the firm policies—if you are truly convinced you could offer a way to improve a process and add value to the firm—watch. Watch the process in a variety of matters over the course of a few months. Try to understand every aspect of it and the documents/communications that flow through it. If after a few months of observation, you still feel as though the process can be improved, develop a plan to improve the process and implement it. But only on a single matter in which you can exert some level of control. If your experiment is successful, break it apart. Why did it work? Can it be broken down into easy-to-follow tasks? Is it something that can be rapidly taught and implemented by many people? Does it require special knowledge of some kind?

If after all has been said and done, you genuinely feel as though you can help improve the efficiency of the workplace, request a meeting with the senior partner responsible for the process. Ask them questions. Why was it set up in this fashion? What is it designed to address? Does he or she have any ideas of how it could be improved? As you engage them on the topic, now is the time to bring out your plan and explain how it works. Explain why you changed the process and why you believe it works better. Depending on the senior attorney this could evoke genuine interest or a brutal cross-examination. Be prepared for both.

Regardless, the senior partner should be impressed by one thing: you care. You're not a mindless drone, coming into work to grind away at your desk. You are attempting to be more productive, help the firm, add value. Yes, doing this will make you stand out in your firm and attract attention—but why do you want to blend in?

The same is true with the contract. Find a treatise on the subject and see what the prevailing trend is across the country. Look at the law generally, then get specific. Dig deep into the case law on point. Find other contracts that are similar to the deal and see how they are structured. If you feel as though an adjustment or improvement can be made after doing your research, call up the person who gave you the contract. Ask them out to lunch or just stop by their office. Ask about the original contract. Why is it structured the way it is? Who wrote it?

You might change the contract, you might not. But you certainly just deepened your knowledge of a certain area of contract law. You also likely strengthened your relationship with the other attorney. You've also shown yourself to be someone who doesn't just take what is handed to them. That you care about the work you do and that you are going to think through matters that come to you—not just process them like a mindless automaton.

Either way, it's an opportunity to begin developing a reputation for yourself. An opportunity to display that you are not a mindless worker bee. An opportunity to show that you are willing to go the extra mile to get the job done right.

ARE YOU A WORKER BEE OR A RENEGADE KILLER BEE?

> That's you, trying to disguise yourself as a worker bee. That's you tryin' to blend in with the hive. But you're not a worker bee. You're a renegade killer bee.
> —Bill, the master assassin, to his protégé, in Quentin Tarintino's film *Kill Bill Volume II*

Too many people who went to law school want to be worker bees and have someone tell them how to do everything and where to do it.

If you're going to be a new lawyer—whether in an established firm or in your own practice—you've got to be a renegade killer bee. Worker bees by their very nature are replaceable. Renegade killer bees are rare. They are valuable. People (firms and clients) need them. If you're just a regular worker bee, wanting to come in and punch the clock, don't be surprised when you don't get a job or clients.

But being a worker bee is easy. It's seductive. Show up and someone hands you something to do. Don't think outside of the box. Stay inside firmly set boundaries. Follow the set path laid before you. Just do the work you are given. No need to go the extra mile. No real responsibilities; no risk.

Being a renegade killer bee is hard. There is no set path. No one is going to hold your hand through it. You might find some assistance here and there when you cross paths with another renegade killer bee, but largely you are on your own. A renegade killer bee is, by its nature, largely on its own. It does not stay with the hive. It does not mindlessly drone on with its work. A renegade killer bee forges new paths and explores new areas. It has to take full responsibility for its actions, assume all the risks with its activities.

You put your ass on the line when you are a renegade killer bee. You have skin in the game. Something riding on what you do. It's the difference between casually watching a football game in the afternoon because it happens to be on television versus sitting on the edge of your seat watching a game because you placed a $1000.00 bet on it. You care when there is risk involved.

Some people are natural renegade killer bees. No one needs to tell them what they need to do, it's just who they are. But there is nothing stopping worker bees from becoming renegade killer bees—they just need to start taking risks. Pushing themselves out of their little drone routine and trying something outside of their comfort zone, something that is challenging and causes them to stretch to reach their goal.

At some point you have to look at the risk, look at the fall you might take, and make the jump anyway.

PERSONAL BRANDING IS STUPID

Reputations are fragile things—intricate, delicate structures that require years to develop and build but only moments to shatter.

Don't exaggerate your life, your experience, or status in order to impress others or win clients. Be honest and upfront about who you are and what you're about. Let your work speak for itself. There is no need to inflate your credentials in order to wow others. Or to assume postures or positions in order to try and "frame" yourself as something you are not.

Believe in your words, believe in yourself. Contribute to ignorance-reduction, not the propagation of the banal and the benign. Take a risk and say what you know needs to be said.

It's what the rest of us really need to hear from you anyway.

Shut up about your "personal brand." A brand is only the first step, the foot in the door. That's it. This sudden obsession with developing a personal brand is insane. No one cares about your personal brand. Let me say that again: **No one gives a damn about your personal brand**. Marketers and social media/branding gurus may say otherwise, but they are merely trying to justify their own existence.

You know what matters for lawyers—anyone really? Their reputation.

Your brand is what you say about yourself, but your reputation is what others say about you.

There is no way to self-create a reputation—or at least no way to buy a reputation that lasts. You can't fake a reputation for very long. Reputation is developed through hard work, consistency, reliability, and integrity.

That last one trips people up. Integrity is not that popular of a word in the 21st century. Look at the general mess of "entertainment" available on television: reality shows, celebrity divorces, back-stabbing politicians. Integrity has seemingly faded from the daily lexicon. But for anyone looking to develop a reputation that matters, integrity is essential.

Integrity does not involve subscribing to some Aristotelian level of ethics. Instead, integrity is unity of behavior in thought, word, and action. Having integrity while consistently and reliably delivering quality work will eventually ensure that other people will speak highly of you—you won't have to do it yourself.

HOW TO CONDUCT YOURSELF ONLINE (OR NOT)

If you are a new lawyer you are online. It's not even like the Internet is a separate space any longer—some foreign thing that needs to be logged in through a terminal. It's not even that the Internet is in our pockets. The Internet is everywhere. Just another part of life, interminable and ever present.

Meaning that any sort of division or separation between the online version of you and the IRL (in real life) version of you is crumbling. Sure you might try to be anonymous online at some obscure message board but you're also going to be active under your real name on Facebook, Twitter, and whatever else pops up in the coming years. The same is doubly true for your firm. You're not going to hide your firm online, hoping no one can find it. You want people to find it. So you Tweet. Post updates on Facebook. Start a blog. Something, anything, to make your presence known.

While the amount of traffic may be low, and your audience small, you should treat anything you post online as though it might be front page news on every newsite the following day—because it could be. While the odds are definitely against it happening, there is a saying in the hacker community: "security through obscurity is no security at all." The same holds true for your words online. Hoping that they are too obscure to notice is setting yourself up to be blindsided. You need to take the same care in how you present your online presence, as you do IRL.

When I started Associate's Mind, I didn't have a particular objective in mind. I had only vague initial goals: explore my thoughts on what it meant to be a young lawyer—and how to become a better one. It seemed the only suitable topic because choosing any specific area of law to cover would have entailed me doing something I'm not comfortable with: pretending to be something that I'm not.

I thought about crafting a blog around a specific niche/practice area, but anything I posted would be conjecture or posturing. There is an argument—one that I agree with—that a person can learn a great deal by writing about a topic. But I wouldn't share that writing if it was on a topic I wasn't familiar with, and I wasn't confident in my ability to discuss it intelligently with other people. So I kept my writing to what I knew: self-improvement, time management, technology, developing relationships, telling stories. Yet many other new lawyers online don't seem to have the same self-restraint.

The ease of publishing that has arisen with the Internet has pros and cons. It readily allows anyone to have a voice—but it also requires readers to have their bullshit detectors set to High as very few people actually have anything worthy to say.

While nominally a blog is for other people to read—I was (and continue to be) selfish—I wanted my blogging to make **me** better professionally and personally. I never felt the need to project some sort of farcical, manicured version of myself online in order to "win friends and influence people," gain clients, or make myself seem more than I am. Yet many new lawyers tailor the image they project of themselves online in order to make themselves seem much larger than they are in real life—in the hopes of appearing to be a "thought leader" or gain traffic or impress potential clients. While it might seem innocent enough, it can have disastrous results. Look no further than the scandal surrounding Joseph Rakofsky.[1]

Joseph Rakofsky was a young lawyer with a big Internet presence. On websites he boasted:

> Mr. Rakofsky has worked on cases involving Murder, Embezzlement, Tax Evasion, Civil RICO, Securities Fraud, Bank Fraud, Insurance Fraud, Wire Fraud, Conspiracy, Money Laundering, Drug Trafficking, Grand Larceny, Identity Theft, Counterfeit Credit

---

1. About which, much was said online: http://blog.bennettandbennett.com/2011/05/compendium-of-rakofsky-v-internet-blog-posts.html

Card Enterprise and Aggravated Harassment. Following graduation from law school, he worked for one of the biggest civil litigation firms on the east coast and has worked for boutique white-collar criminal defense firms in Manhattan.[2]

All within less than a year of practice! Rakofsky also had numerous websites, online videos, and profiles on attorney listing services that funneled visitors back to the main website of his solo practice.

Eventually, all his web marketing worked! Rakofsky got a client. A criminal client. A criminal client accused of First Degree Murder. So what happened?

A Washington, D.C., judge declared a mistrial in a murder case Friday, saying he was "astonished" at the performance of the defense lawyer who confessed to jurors he'd never tried a case before.

Judge William Jackson said lawyer Joseph Rakofsky did not have a good grasp of legal procedures, citing as an example the attorney's rambling opening statement in which he told of his inexperience, the Washington Post reports. Rakofsky graduated from Touro law school in 2009 and obtained a law license in New Jersey less than a year ago, the story says.

Rakofsky had repeated disagreements with his local D.C. counsel, causing his client, Dontrell Deaner, to become "visibly frustrated," the Post says. On Friday, Deaner told the judge he wanted a new lawyer.

The judge declared a mistrial after reviewing a court filing in which an investigator had claimed Rakofsky fired him for refusing to carry out the lawyer's emailed suggestion to "trick" a witness, the story says. Rakofsky's suggestion allegedly read: "Thank you for your help. Please trick the old lady to say that

_____

2. http://unwashedadvocate.com/2011/04/04/lying-piece-of-with-screenshot-as-evidence/

she did not see the shooting or provide information to
the lawyers about the shooting."[3]

In Judge Jackson's exact words: "I believe that the performance was below
what any reasonable person would expect in a murder trial." If that wasn't
enough, after the case was dismissed, Rakofsky hopped onto Facebook
and bragged that he had "obtained" a mistrial (in which the client had to
spend a year or so in pretrial confinement waiting on the retrial).

Rakofsky's incompetent handling of the case led to stories in the
Washington Post, Reuters, and the ABA Journal. Within days, dozens
of legal blogs had reported on the story and expressed opinions on the
outcome, the ethical issues raised, and the dangers of retaining a lawyer
based on exaggerated marketing. But after a couple of weeks, the story
faded away. It would have always been a black mark on Rakofsky, but
something that he could have mollified. Rakofsky had the opportunity
to learn from his mistake, dedicate himself to handling lesser matters,
growing in small steps, and learning to become a better attorney away
from the limelight. Instead, Rakofsky doubled down and began what
came to be known as Rakofsky v. The Internet.[4]

Rakofsky sued the aforementioned media outlets, as well as the
American Bar Association, Above The Law, and dozens of other legal
blogs, totaling over eighty defendants in all. The complaint alleged
numerous causes of action ranging from injurious falsehood to the
completely non-existent "cyber-mobbing." The lawsuit was, of course,
frivolous. The media outlets were merely reporting on the proceedings
of the court, as were the legal blogs that commented on the lawsuit.
Despite the spurious nature of Rakofsky's claims, the lawsuit dragged
out over two years and thousands of pages of motion practice. All the
while, news outlets continued to report on the ludicrous nature of the
lawsuit and the self-destructive actions of Joseph Rakofsky. In early
2013, the lawsuit came to an end when the presiding judge issued an
order granting the defendants' motion to dismiss all causes of action.
All of Rakofsky's bluster and lawsuits amounted to nothing. All he got

---

3. Debra Cassens Weiss, *'Astonished' Judge Declares Murder Mistrial Due to
Lawyer who Never Tried a Case*, ABA JOURNAL (Apr. 4, 2011, 6:00 a.m.), http://www
.abajournal.com/news/article/astonished_judge_declares_murder_mistrial_cites
_inexperienced_lawyer_who_ne.

4. Credit to Scott Greenfield for this naming convention.

in the end was his name associated with the worst sort of behavior in which a new lawyer could be engaged. All from pretending to be something more than he really was.

The lesson to be gained from Rakofsky v. The Internet is that a new lawyer needs to resist the temptation to make spurious and unfounded claims as to their capabilities and experience. There will be many companies and people out there who will encourage you otherwise. Lawyer rating services, directories, marketing gurus, and social media coaches who will tell you that it is okay to be aggressive and puff up your online presence. They will show you how you can make sure that what you put up just fits in with ethical guidelines. But the ethical rules are not the high bar of conduct for an ethical lawyer—they are the baseline, the ground floor minimum from which to begin.

The truth is that a lawyer's online behavior needs be no different than how they conduct themselves in any other setting. Honesty, integrity, and a forthrightness about who you are—and who you are not—is essential if you wish to build trust with others. Again, when I started Associate's Mind, I was simply myself. No puffery, no vagueness regarding who I was or what I was trying to do. Yet within six months after I started Associate's Mind, it went from having zero presence online to one of the fifty most popular legal blogs out of the almost 500 tracked by Avvo.com. The following year Associate's Mind was selected as part of the ABA Journal's Blawg 100. Associate's Mind has been linked to by the *Wall Street Journal*, appeared in The Browser, and showed up on Reddit now and again. I bring this up not to boast, but to point out that I succeeded in the legal blogging world without having to pretend to be something that I am not.

No SEO, no social media strategy, no puffery or marketing. None of that crap because it isn't necessary. It's not about the ancillary methods a person uses to deliver their message online—the message is what matters.

I was never "faking it til I made it." I was up front that I was a recent law graduate who was taking his initial steps in the profession; publicly exploring my thoughts and ideas on how to conduct oneself as a new lawyer. I still am. I'm on the same journey of professional development as you are.

Hopefully you'll want to ride alongside me for part of the way there. And I shouldn't to have to trick you into doing it.

BUSY V. REMARKABLE

One day I was corresponding with a friend and the topic of extra-curricular projects came up. I rattled off a list of six or seven things I was doing outside of my practice: Bar committees, speaking engagements, article writing, etc. (writing a book!). All of them, taken with the day-in, day-out grind of being a lawyer, can sometimes lead me to be fairly busy. But I'm also careful to not be too busy. I have found that when I am too busy, stretched too thin, activities or projects inevitably suffer.

Which leads me back to the work of Dr. Cal Newport. In Dr. Newport's advocacy of developing significant, valuable skills, he places a large emphasis on "deep work." Deep work is cognitively demanding activity that leverages a person's training to generate rare and valuable results, and that push their abilities to continually improve.[1] It's important to qualify and acknowledge that deep work exists and is separate from "shallow work." Much of what takes place in a given workday is likely to be shallow work.

Shallow work is replying to emails, administrative planning, talking on the phone. Worrying about supplies, managing inter-office politics, reading a memo. Cumulatively, they are all the little things that eat up large parts of your day. Dr. Newport notes that this work is often attractive because it's easy, which in turn makes people feel productive. It's also often rich in personal interaction, which most people enjoy.

Yet deep work is where we produce the most value. For lawyers, deep work is analysis, deconstructing arguments, writing briefs. It is not "busy" work. It is quiet work, something that requires planning and time to be set aside. As Dr. Newport notes:

> Deep work is phasic . . . we're not computer processors.

---

1. Cal Newport, *Knowledge Workers are Bad at Working (And Here's what to Do About It…)*, STUDY HACKS (Nov. 21, 2012, 5:16 p.m.), http://calnewport.com/blog/2012/11/21/knowledge-workers-are-bad-at-working-and-heres-what-to-do-about-it/.

We can't be expected to accomplish any job any time we have the available cycles. There are rhythms to our psychology. Certain times of the day, week, month, and even year are better suited for deep work than other times.

To respect this reality, you must leave sufficient time in your schedule to handle the intense bursts of such work when they occur. This requires that you constrain the other obligations in your life—perhaps by being reluctant to agree to things or start projects, or by ruthlessly batching and streamlining your regular obligations.

When it's time to work deeply, this approach leaves you the schedule space necessary to immerse.

I've found this to be very true in regards to my own productivity and that of many other lawyers I speak with. There are certain times of the day, certain times of the week, when I find that I can just work. I know that if I sit down at my computer from 7:00 to 10:00 a.m., whether it be writing motions or articles or letters, I can plow through them with ease. If I try write in the afternoon, the quality inevitably suffers. It's not that I can't or won't write in the afternoon or evening, but I know that I can much more easily slip into a state of deep work when I am in a certain place, at a certain time.

Taking the time to discover when you are best capable of deep work is something that is incredibly important if you want to produce remarkable work. There is no guarantee that you will produce something remarkable, but you will increase your chances of producing such a thing if you know when you are most capable, most open to letting go of everything else in your life—responsibilities, bills, deadlines—and focusing on a single task or problem.

It often seems incredibly difficult to let things go in today's always on, always connected world. There is a desire to multi-task and switch gears at all times. Check Twitter, check email, review a letter. Write a couple paragraphs in brief, get phone call. While on phone, pull up Facebook. Phone call ends, check Twitter, back to brief. Another lawyer sticks his head in your office, wants to talk about an issue in a different case. Finish conversation, back to brief, an urgent email notification pops up. Read email, not really that urgent. Reply anyway. Couple more paragraphs into brief, calendar notification goes off. Lunch scheduled with another lawyer in twenty-five minutes.

Maybe some people can be productive in such an environment or schedule. Or rather, I'm sure they feel as though they are productive. But as Newport points out, we are not computers. We don't actually juggle processes in the background and switch tasks at will. It takes time—uninterrupted time—to get into a mode of deep work. Constant interruptions and distractions only serve to chip away at your ability to go deep and produce remarkable results.

So discover when you are the most productive. Whittle away your responsibilities from that time. Let it be open. Even if you have nothing particularly pressing to do, keep that time free. It is potential. Ready to be filled with your work when you need it.

HOW YOU CONFRONT YOUR DAY IS YOUR CHOICE

Starting out one's career as a lawyer is hard. You're inexperienced, with only a passing knowledge of the law, thrust into being responsible for other people's problems. Too often you might not feel confident in handling your own. People are going to be apt to criticize you for any mistake you might make and take you to task for not handling a matter exactly as they would have wished. When beset with criticism and difficult situations it can be easy to turn inwards and reel in feelings of doubt and self-confidence. It can be difficult to preserve. Yet, how we deal with problems is largely of our own choosing. It is a position you can find in the advice of many people.

- "The pessimist sees difficulty in every opportunity. The optimist sees the opportunity in every difficulty." —Winston Churchill
- "Every wall is a door." —Ralph Waldo Emerson
- "You cannot tailor make the situations in life, but you can tailor make the attitudes to fit those situations before they arise." —Zig Ziglar

This is a simple truth that most people fail to grasp. People want to place their feelings, moods, and attitude at the feet of others.

- "My husband stayed at the office too late so I am resentful."
- "My leg is broken so I am sad."
- "I don't have a job so I'm angry at law school."

People regularly let other people, places, and things determine their own mental state. People give others control over how they feel. They allow it to happen out of habit, but ultimately it is a choice that they make.

Kevin Blok, the instructor I studied under for a year while I was an *uchi deshi*, often speaks on this choice. There is one story in particular he tells that lays out this choice in very clear terms. Here is the following story from his perspective, as he has told it to thousands of others.

*****

I was in my twenties when I decided to dedicate my life to martial arts. I spent a significant amount of time in China and Japan during this time. Sometimes traveling with others, sometimes by myself. On one trip, I had been reading about a zen intensive at a remote mountain monastery. Ten days submerged in the life of a monk. I tried to get some of my friends to go with me, but they balked because it was expensive. Thousands of dollars. They told me I was crazy for wanting to spend that much money to live in a monastery for ten days. So I made plans to go on the intensive myself, while they made plans to go spend a week in Taiwan partying.

But I knew what I was doing! I was going to go get me some enlightenment! I'd go up on the mountain for ten days and come down wise and full of knowledge. As should be apparent, I was young, stupid, and didn't know what I was in for.

I arrived at the monastery and was immediately stripped of all my possessions—even my clothes. I was given a very thin robe to wear, the same as everyone else. It was quite cold on top of the mountain. Being cold came to define much of my time there. As did hunger, work, and pain.

The first thing I did was work, placed in the fields in which the monastery grew all their food. Up and down the rows, shoveling, raking, or harvesting. And while it was back-breaking work, it came to be a respite as the rest of the day was spent in meditation.

Most Westerners have a very misguided, romanticized idea of meditation. Meditation is not incense, soft lights, pillows, and new age music. Traditional zen meditation is hours sitting in *seiza*. No sound, no movement. Complete silence and stillness. Ideally, you empty your mind and embrace it. In practice, it is incredibly frustrating and aggravating. And it's compounded by the fact that the abbot in charge of meditation walks up and down the meditation hall, carrying a large stick. If at any point in time he thinks you aren't focusing correctly he comes behind you and strikes you—hard—across your shoulders.

I got hit a lot.

Outside of working or meditation, the only other activity was meals. Now, I'm a big guy, and at this time young and very physically fit. I normally consumed a lot of food in any given meal. But at the monastery, the diet was vegetarian—and not much of it. Generally speaking it was rice, some few vegetables and broth-like soup. All consumed in silence like the rest of the day.

To say it was awful is an understatement. But I had paid in advance and there were no refunds, so I was determined to stay. So I farmed and sat, day-in, day-out. I spent the nights curled up under a thin blanket, sleeping on a stone floor, cursing myself for choosing to do something so stupid.

About ¾ of the way through the intensive, the abbot took us outside and sat us down in the garden and told us we were going to engage in a different type of meditation today. This perked me up because anything was going to be a reprieve from the drudgery that was life in the monastery.

The abbot walked around and passed out a small mirror to everyone. He told us we were to engage in "laughter meditation." For the next twenty minutes, we were to sit and look into the mirror and laugh.

This was the most ridiculous concept I had ever heard of. But if I didn't laugh, the abbot would begin hitting me with his stick. So away I laughed.

"Ha.Ha.Ha." I laughed, flat and annoyed. The most insincere laugh I could muster. Completely and totally fake. I can do this for twenty minutes.

Sitting there laughing at my face in the mirror, I couldn't help but think about how **stupid** all this was. My friends are in Taiwan. They're likely drinking, going out, meeting girls. They aren't cold, hungry, and in pain. Minutes go by while I laugh my fake laugh at my reflection.

My mind starts to go to the money I spent on this—thousands of dollars to be wretched. On the pathetic amounts of food I'm eating. What I would give for a hamburger! Farming and sitting. Being hit again and again by some old man. It was crazy! I was crazy for doing it! What a ridiculous situation I put myself in. Then I look at myself again—really look at myself—sitting in a garden, holding a mirror laughing at my reflection. It's hilarious the situation I'm in! Paying to be miserable!? I start laughing at me. Like really laughing at myself. The more I think about it, the funnier it becomes.

The laughter just starts pouring out of me and I can't stop it. That type of deep laughter that causes your chest to clinch and makes you lose your breath. Soon, I'm just crying I'm laughing so hard. Tears are streaming down my face. The sheer absurdity of the entire situation. How bizarre and comical it was that I had come to the other side of the world and spent thousands of dollars to be miserable. I couldn't help but laugh and laugh and laugh.

And what had changed???

Why was I now so happy???

I was still cold. Still hungry, sore, and in pain from long stints of sitting and being beaten across my back. Still out thousands of dollars and time away from my friends. Nothing had changed about my situation. The only thing that changed was my mind. That I looked at my situation and just laughed at it instead.

When the laughter meditation was done, we went back to our regular schedule. The rest of my time there was great. I happily toiled away in the field. Smiled when the abbot hit me with his stick.

I didn't become enlightened from the time I spent at that monastery—but I did learn that how I interact with the world, my mindset, my attitude—is **mine** to control. It's not dictated by other people, or my situation, or the things I do or don't have. It's an internal thing. It comes from the inside out.

*****

It's simple, straightforward advice. But simple does not mean easy. If it was easy, then the world would be filled with happy people. It is a hard choice to be happy and approach life with a positive mental attitude. It's something that you try and fail at much of the time. I know I certainly do. But there is little else in life of which we have control.

That's not to say that you move through life putting on a happy mask in the worst of situations. There are going to be bad times. Dark times. Especially as a lawyer. As I stated previously, becoming a good lawyer requires failure. That's the nature of the game. You are going to fail. Beyond that, you are going to lose. You will be a loser. On a motion, or an arbitration, a contract dispute, merger clause, or conviction. You. Are. Going. To. Lose.

It will hurt. Hurt your pride and piss you off. Especially when you lose on some procedural rule over which you had no control. Or when some hidden evidence or witness makes an appearance at the 11th hour. I distinctly recall an appellate brief whose argument I knew was a winner, and the appellate court agreed, but the court stated the record on appeal didn't have enough evidence to support it, which I knew was likely going to happen as the case was over a decade old, and missing much of the older evidence. But to be told that, yes you have a good argument, but no you can't win, was infuriating. I was in a foul mood for the rest of the day.

Yet on the next day, I had to set it aside. There were other cases and other clients that needed my attention—not my moping. I had to take my beating and move on to the next battle. Crying over spilt milk, wallowing in your lot in life, accomplishes absolutely nothing. It is wasted energy. Not to say that on occasion you won't want to drown your sorrows and be dragged down by the world for a time. But be mad, frustrated, cry, whatever—then let it go.

Letting other people, your cases, or the world control your attitude does you no good. It lessens your ability to do significant work. It is a disservice to your clients, to your family, to yourself. Deciding to approach law, life, your family and friends, with openness and positivity, despite the setbacks and obstacles in your path, is a powerful tool. Do not allow negativity that comes your way to derail you from your goals or control how you feel.

So when you wake up tomorrow morning, try to remember that whether or not you have a good day is largely left up to you.

Make the most of it.

THERE HAS NEVER BEEN A BETTER TIME TO BE A LAWYER

Banker A: The markets are terrible. There is no predictability. Everything is unstable. It's so hard to make money. This is the worst time ever to be trading. What can we do? I hate the market right now.

Banker B: I love the market.

Banker A: WHAT?!? How can you? It's so bad right now. Like this? Are you crazy? The market is horrible right now (etc.).

Banker B: You know of another one? I don't. It's the only one we've got. Getting upset about it isn't doing you any good. There's always going to be opportunities, you just have to work hard to find them. So learn to love it or leave it.

Banker A: . . .

What's true in finance is true in the legal field—so carpe diem.

Decades go by in which things are flat and there isn't any change. People trudge by in their jobs and go through the motions at work. There isn't any innovation, creative thinking, or demands on efficiency or productivity. This ain't one of those decades.

The practice of law is in an incredible state of flux. But in times of great change, there are also great opportunities. You just have to be ready to move quickly when they present themselves. There are a number of things you can do to be prepared:

- Pay attention to the news outside of the legal world. Be sensitive to the overall business climate in relation to your clients. This means caring about things like industry trends, the housing market, or local zoning laws. You can't bury your head in the sand. You are supposed to be an educated professional. People come to you for guidance and counseling. You need to be able to explain things in a way that places them in context with what else is going on in the world.

- Immerse yourself deep in the study of your niche area of practice—then study an ancillary one. You need to have deep understanding of your practice area, but if you study it to the exclusion of everything else it can become easy to become too focused. Studying ancillary fields will help provide perspective on your practice.

- Learn about technology, embrace it. Don't be left behind because you think it's not for you. Utilize what makes sense for your practice; abandon what does not. But don't get caught up chasing after the latest shiny toy. Technology is just a tool, what matters is how you use it.

- Develop exceptional personal relationship skills. Write handwritten notes. Reply to calls and emails promptly. Be genuine. Put other people first—especially your clients.

- Get out of the office. Go to Bar events. Go to places where your clients will be: trade shows, associations, the local watering hole, whatever.

- Grow—intellectually and physically. Read challenging works and learn from the Classics. Join a book club. Start an exercise program. Join a gym. Find a hobby. You'll gain new perspectives on the world, be more interesting, and meet new people.

CHANCE FAVORS THE PREPARED

Position yourself so that you can seize an opportunity when it arises. Feeling sorry for yourself or the economy or job market is probably the most useless thing you could be doing with your time. Again, don't wait for opportunities to fall into your lap; **create your own opportunities**. Let everyone else lament over the state of the economy or jobs or whatever else—stick to improving yourself, your practice, and providing high quality, innovative, and timely services. While others are busy crying over spilled milk, you can be the lawyer people will be turning to when they're in need.

It's a crazy time to be a lawyer. I wouldn't have it any other way.

AFTERWORD

Hopefully you have been able to steal something from this book and make it your own. If you'd like to continue to grow and develop as a new lawyer, I invite you to join me and the rest of the community at *http://www.associatesmind.com*. As I've noted through the book, I'm continuing to grow as a new lawyer as well. I hope you will become a part of the community at Associate's Mind and I can steal something from you.

I'm always open to questions and contact from new lawyers trying to find their footing in the profession. You can reach me at keith@associatesmind.com. For quick questions, you can find me on Twitter at http://twitter.com/associatesmind.

If you're curious about learning about the actual business of running a law practice, keep an eye out for my next book coming in the Fall of 2014—"What Can A Lawyer Learn From A MBA?"—a collaboration with a management consultant who has been advising businesses for years.

ACKNOWLEDGMENTS

I could not be where I am today without the input, help, and guidance of a number of people. First and foremost, I would like to acknowledge my parents for everything they have done for me. You have provided love, discipline, and wisdom. Thank you.

I would like to thank Van Bushnell for introducing me to martial arts, and to Kevin Blok for taking me under his wing and showing me the Way. *Osu.*

Law school was a blur, but a number of fellow students stand out. To Patti's basement study crew: thanks for helping me grind it out. Thanks also to Professor Theibert for allowing me to share his Rule #1 story—you've been selected professor of the year by the student body for over seventeen years for a reason.

I'd like to thank Michael Fish for giving me an opportunity when I was just a clueless law student and allowing me to come into his firm and see the inside of the practice.

Since starting Associate's Mind, I've been fortunate enough to become friends with a number of lawyers across the country who have all had an impact on my development as a lawyer. I'd like to thank Mark Bennett, Brian Tannenbaum, and Ken White for sharing their experience so freely. Scott Greenfield who continues to go above and beyond in providing an example of what it means to be a good lawyer. Dan Hull for his raw nature and allowing me to share his 12 Rules. And a special shout out to David Lat and Elie Mystal at ATL for showing Associate's Mind support over the years.

Thanks to Cal Newport for sharing his deconstruction of what it mean to engage in deliberate practice and sharing his research.

To my partners at Hamer Law Group: Chris Hamer and Alan Duke. Chris: you are addicted to hustle—awesome. Alan: you better have written your book by the time this comes out.

Finally, I'd like to thank my editor, Jonathan Malysiak, for his advice and encouragement, and helping the ABA forge a new path in the 21st century.

RESOURCES

The following are a variety of resources I have found useful over the years. While the books will remain available indefinitely, the Internet is tumultuous at best. Some of these communities and blogs could be gone in a year, or they may last another ten years. As a matter of disclosure, I am acquaintances or friends with many of the lawyers who run these blogs and communities. That I am friends with them does not dictate their inclusion. I valued their content long before I came to know them due to their providing news, commentary, information, and analysis that I found to be useful.

BOOKS

GENERAL PRACTICE

Managing The Professional Service Firm (David H. Maister)—A guide on how effective professional service firms run.

The Curmudgeon's Guide To Practicing Law (Mark Herrmann)—A no-nonsense view of practicing law from a partner's perspective. Don't expect belly rubs.

WRITING

Making Your Case (Antonin Scalia & Bryan Garner)—A handbook on making your writing palatable for judges.

Point Made (Ross Guberman)—Provides a strategic roadmap for writing briefs, with hundreds of examples from some of the nation's top advocates.

Writing to Win (Steven Stark)—Probably the best general overview of legal writing available.

ONLINE

CRIMINAL LAW

A Public Defender (http://apublicdefender.com/)—Opinion on the criminal law system from an anonymous public defender.

Defending People (http://blog.bennettandbennett.com/)—Mark Bennett on the tao of criminal-defense trial lawyering.

Simple Justice (http://blog.simplejustice.us/)—Scott Greenfield pontificates on crime, blawgs, the legal industry, or whatever else floats his boat that morning. Prolific and always worth reading.

The Agitator (http://www.huffingtonpost.com/news/the -agitator)—Radley Balko's continuing crusade at uncovering overreach of the government in the areas of civil liberties and the criminal justice system.

The Criminal Lawyer (http://burneylawfirm.com/blog/)—When Nathan Burney is not too busy churning out funny and informative legal comics at www.lawcomic.net, he shares his views on criminal law here.

Unwashed Advocate (http://unwashedadvocate.com/)—Eric Mayer generally discusses military criminal law issues but also veers into Bat Country.

FREE SPEECH AND OTHER CENSORIOUS BEHAVIOR

Popehat (http://www.popehat.com/)—A group complaint about law, liberty, and leisure.

The Legal Satyricon (http://randazza.wordpress.com/)—
Occasionally irreverent thoughts on law, liberty, tech, and politics.

Adam Steinbaugh (http://adamsteinbaugh.com/)—Every other
listing here is alphabetical but Adam goes last in this section
because he was pompous enough to use his name for his blog's
url. Lulz. Read him anyway.

GENERAL PRACTICE

At Counsel Table (http://atcounseltable.com/)—Alex Craigie
shares his views on the craft and business of the courtroom lawyer from the perspective of an AmLaw 200 firm.

Lawyerist (http://lawyerist.com/)—Focused on the nuts and bolts
of practice. Features a stable of rotating contributors.

Litigation and Trial (http://www.litigationandtrial.com/)—
Max Kennerly offers news and opinion from the perspective of a
high end plaintiff's firm.

My Shingle (http://myshingle.com/)—Carolyn Elefant's long running blog on solo practice. Great resource if you are looking to
start a solo practice.

New York Personal Injury Law Blog (http://www
.newyorkpersonalinjuryattorneyblog.com/)—Eric Turkewitz on
interesting civil cases. Nominally New York focused but covers
cases nationwide.

Philly Law Blog (http://phillylawblog.wordpress.com/)—
The Hardy Boys practice law. Represent.

The Trial Warrior (http://thetrialwarrior.com/)—Antonin Pribetic
shares his views on practice and law from a Canadian perspective.

Virtual Law Practice (http://virtuallawpractice.org/)—
Stephanie Kimbro, perhaps the only person online talking about
operating a non-physical (virtual) practice in an ethical and
competent manner.

What About Clients? (http://www.whataboutclients.com/)—
Dan Hull, biz litigator. Posts on life, the universe, and everything.
Focus on client service and the benefits of studying the Classics.

NEWS

ABA Journal (http://www.abajournal.com/)—Broadly covers trends in law and generally perceived as one of the central voices of the legal industry by the mainstream media.

Above The Law (www.abovethelaw.com)—What was once a "legal tabloid" has slowly morphed into the preeminent source of much of today's legal news. Topics range from the inner workings of the largest law firms in the world to guidance for solo practitioners and law school rankings.

Overlawyered (http://overlawyered.com/)—One of the oldest running law blogs. Covers the legal system as a whole.

SCOTUSblog (http://www.scotusblog.com/)—Discussion of recent developments in U.S. Supreme Court jurisprudence.

Wall Street Journal Law Blog (http://blogs.wsj.com/law/)—The Street's view of the legal industry.

WRITING

CopyBlogger (http://www.copyblogger.com/)—Developing marketing copy that leads to conversions. Translation: Writing so well and persuasively that the incessantly-clicking, ADHD, driven-to-distraction masses will actually purchase something. If you want to see high quality persuasive writing, look no further.

LawProse (http://www.lawprose.org/blog/)—Bryan Garner's blog. Provides daily usage tips for words and phrases. For aspiring snoots.

Legal Skills Prof Blog (http://lawprofessors.typepad.com/legal_skills/)—Often about general legal skills and news related to the profession, but features writing specific posts regularly.

Legal Writing Prof Blog (http://lawprofessors.typepad.com/legalwriting/)—General tips on writing from a law professor perspective. Often links to Law Review articles on writing.

LegalWritingPro (http://legalwritingpro.com/)—Ross Guberman, George Washington University Law Prof, author of *Point Made*. Regular articles on writing.

LegalWriting.net (http://blogs.utexas.edu/legalwriting/)—Wayne Scheiss, Texas School of Law professor and author of four books on legal writing. Posts sporadically, but always good reading.

Manage Your Writing (http://www.manageyourwriting.com/)—Ken Davis, former English prof turned biz writing consultant. Focused on business writing, but provides useful general writing tips.

The Appellate Record (http://www.appellaterecord.com/)—Kendall Gray, Texas appellate lawyer. Often focused on Texas, but regularly provides insights on appellate writing.

The (new) Legal Writer (http://raymondpward.typepad.com/newlegalwriter/)—Raymond Ward, Louisiana appellate lawyer. Posts infrequently, but always good advice.

ABOUT THE AUTHOR

Keith Robert Lee tried a little bit of everything before he decided what he wanted to do. He has had jobs cleaning dishes, mowing golf courses, washing cars, engraving brass, stocking library bookshelves, and making video games. When it seemed like it was time to do something more concrete, Keith got his undergraduate degree from the University of Alabama at Birmingham—but recalls that most of that time was actually spent not at college.

Keith then lived in a closet in the basement of a martial arts school because it seemed like a good idea at the time. He went on to teach martial arts across the United States, Canada, and an occasional seminar in Europe.

After that experience, law school didn't seem like it could be that bad. So Keith enrolled at Birmingham School of Law. Law school had its ups and downs but led to a great number of great friendships that seem just as important now as the law degree. While in law school, he founded Associate's Mind, which became one of the most popular legal blogs in the United States, despite whatever Keith seemed to be doing to it.

Keith practices law at Hamer Law Group in Birmingham, Alabama. At this point, it seems as though he is going to stick to being a lawyer—but no promises. He lives with his wife, Charlene, and their son, Aidan, who continue to be an inspiration.

INDEX